JK
1061
L8

Luce, R.
Congress

Date Due

CALIFORNIA STATE COLLEGE
SAN BERNARDINO LIBRARY
5500 State College Parkway
San Bernardino, Calif. 92407

PRINTED IN U.S.A.

CONGRESS
AN EXPLANATION

LONDON : HUMPHREY MILFORD

OXFORD UNIVERSITY PRESS

CONGRESS

AN EXPLANATION

By ROBERT LUCE

REPRESENTATIVE OF THE THIRTEENTH DISTRICT
OF MASSACHUSETTS

*Being Five Lectures delivered at Harvard University
in March and April, 1925, on the
Godkin Foundation*

CAMBRIDGE
HARVARD UNIVERSITY PRESS
1926

COPYRIGHT, 1926
BY THE PRESIDENT AND FELLOWS OF
HARVARD COLLEGE

PRINTED AT THE HARVARD UNIVERSITY PRESS
CAMBRIDGE, MASS., U.S.A.

FOREWORD

SHORTLY after the death of Edwin Lawrence Godkin, founder of the New York *Nation* and for many years its editor, some of his friends, inspired by a desire to express their admiration and gratitude for his long and distinguished service to the country of his adoption, endowed the Godkin Lectures, in order to perpetuate his name and stimulate that spirit of independent thought and unselfish devotion to the public good which, they believed, had characterized his life and distinguished his career. They thereby intended to provide for the delivery and publication of lectures upon the essentials of free government and the duties of the citizen by lecturers of the highest distinction. In furtherance of their purpose Congressman Luce was invited to deliver the lectures, which with appropriate changes are printed in this volume.

Congressman Luce's fitness for the task needs no other proof than is afforded by the lectures themselves. His many years of service in the Massachusetts General Court, in the office of Lieutenant-Governor, and in the Constitutional Convention of 1917-18, together with his subsequent service in the Congress of the United States, have given him an exceptional opportunity for the study of free government and the duties of citizenship, which he has already turned to good account in the preparation of his works on *Legislative Assemblies* and *Legislative Procedure*. If the present volume should do no more than promote a wider interest in Congressman Luce's other works, it would accomplish its part in gratifying the desire of those who endowed the Godkin Lectures. But to those who may be unable to read the larger works, and to others also, this little book can convey much of the fruits of its author's ripened studies and wide experience.

ARTHUR N. HOLCOMBE
Professor of Government

HARVARD UNIVERSITY

CONTENTS

LECTURE I
THE GENESIS OF A STATUTE 3

LECTURE II
LAWS AND EXCEPTIONS 33

LECTURE III
SPENDING PUBLIC MONEY 63

LECTURE IV
LEADERSHIP 94

LECTURE V
CRITICISM AND REMEDY 124

CONGRESS
AN EXPLANATION

Lecture I

THE GENESIS OF A STATUTE

LEGISLATORS conceive few of the great mass of statutes enacted every year. This is particularly true of Congressmen, because for the most part they have passed the inventing stage. Experience has made them sceptical. Their instincts are hostile to change. The negative attitude is really their danger. To be sure, a few see in presenting bills a chance to make political capital for personal ends. A few others are unselfishly anxious to better social or industrial or commercial conditions. Yet for by far the greater part of the 15,000 and more of proposals laid before each Congress nowadays, Senators and Representatives are merely conduits, the means of transmission, and for very many of them they are not even endorsers to the extent of guaranteeing more than perfunctory interest. The true source may usually be found in some administrative official, or in some organization, or in some constituent with a grievance, an ambition, or a hope. Congress is not to any material extent an originating body.

Probably more than half the business, measured by importance, comes directly or indirectly from the

Departments or Bureaus of the government. The allegation that Congress itself wilfully seeks to interfere with the executive branch and of its own initiative harries the various offices by legislation, is quite contrary to the facts.

It would, of course, be out of the question for Senate or House to pass judgment forthwith on each of the thousands of proposals presented. Hence the resort to committees. They are denounced. They are dubbed "little legislatures." They are said to be undemocratic. But they are the product of American experience, and we think they furnish the best way to handle the work of initial study and selection.

Englishmen think otherwise. They do not use standing committees like ours. With them the decision as to what public bills Parliament shall consider, rests with that small group of its members known as the Cabinet. Private bills go to committees, but all the big enactments result from winnowing and perfecting by the ministers of the moment. The reason is clear and simple. The ministry must, from start to finish, be responsible for every important piece of legislation. Its very life depends on approval by a majority of the House at every step. It could not run the risk of having a committee report something obnoxious to its policies or purposes.

The English method is so tied up with the Cabinet system that it cannot to much good be contrasted

THE GENESIS OF A STATUTE

with ours. Perhaps the bills introduced by the British Government are in better technical shape than our bills when reported from committees, but naturally they have been framed from only the bureaucratic point of view. When we take a bill draughted by a Department or Bureau, as we often do, we modify it to suit our own ideas. Thus we carry out at any rate the purpose of representative government. To be sure, the same purpose is sought in Parliament by amendment on the floor of the House; but that is a clumsy process at best. There is gain in having a bill perfected in point of principle as much as possible before reaching the floor, and committee work helps toward this.

Our way has the advantage of creating groups of specialists. Committee members gradually acquire a valuable fund of information bearing on the topics handled. In the course of years they become familiar with the history of the field concerned. By observing the officials with whom they frequently come in contact, they learn whom to trust and how far confidence can be put in advice. Sometimes they become better informed than the heads of departments themselves. Often they make wiser judgments in matters of policy, because they have a broader outlook, a better understanding of the needs of the country as a whole, more sense of proportion. Bureaucrats unconsciously magnify their own activities. Committee members check extravagance and save the taxpayers many millions.

It has been suggested that the torrent of bills poured into committee hoppers could be greatly lessened by the use of a sifting committee to exercise in advance the power of selection. In view of the specialized knowledge of committees, and particularly of the chairman (the majority member who has served longest), it is improbable that a sifting committee would exercise as good judgment as is now secured. The trouble with all conglomerate committees handling a wide range of subjects is that only one or two members are likely to have any particular knowledge of any particular topic. The specialized committee commands better judgment in its own field.

Whatever the theories, there is not the least likelihood that the American committee system will in our day be abandoned or materially changed, so profit comes only from observing how it works.

In Congress the Senate has 34 committees, nearly all functioning, for it has reformed its organization. The House has 61, about two thirds of which get something to do, the rest being superfluities, sustained for ulterior but not altogether useless purposes. A score of the House Committees do nine tenths of the work.

How they shall be chosen has been a bone of con-

THE GENESIS OF A STATUTE

tention and still causes grumbling. In the First Congress the House decided that the Speaker should name the committees rather than have them named from the floor or chosen by ballot, which had been the common practices in parliamentary bodies prior thereto. Designation by the Speaker continued until 1911, when election was substituted in the revolt against the Speaker's power. Nothing like a real election followed. The Republicans prevented it as far as their members were concerned by creating a Committee on Committees, chosen by their caucus, and the Democrats achieved the same result by entrusting the task to their members of the Committee on Ways and Means. Some men who were in the House when it worked under the old plan think that nothing has been gained by the change. After all, it is not a matter of the consequence to the country that public discussion has given to it, however much it may affect individual fortunes. Custom lets a member once assigned to a committee stay on it as long as he pleases, and as comparatively few men seek a shift, the opening of each new Congress finds few more problems presented than those resulting from the change nowadays of about one quarter of the membership of the House. In Washington but little can be known of the qualities of the newcomers, and anyhow they may or may not prove suited to the peculiar needs of Congressional work.

So the wisdom of their allotment is largely a matter of chance, and who shall make the decisions is of no great moment. The really objectionable feature of the present method is that it does not place in the hands of one strong man the responsibility for action when changes put in line for an important chairmanship somebody well known to be incompetent or, at least, to be not the most competent.

The embarrassments in such a situation are the inevitable results of the system of promotion by seniority of service, which gets sharp criticism from outside. Nobody can deny its defects. Besides sometimes bringing dangerous power to weak men, it sometimes works mischief the other way round, by keeping down distinctly strong men. An unkind fate may block a promising career by putting a new member on a committee below seniors in service who hold on tenaciously for many years. Inasmuch as it is the chairmanship that ensures an easy opportunity for prominence in the floor work of the House, hard luck may in this way disappoint the ambitious man. Incidentally it will shut him out of the additional office room and clerical help that go with the chairmanship of the working committees. The thoughtless will, of course, promptly say that all this could be easily avoided by disregarding seniority and naming the best man for chairman. They can have had little or no experience with pre-

THE GENESIS OF A STATUTE

cisely the same problem in the conduct of every sizeable business enterprise, or any sort of organization where occasion arises to promote employees. On the whole, the men who must there decide find that promotion by seniority conduces most to contentment and least endangers morale. Exceptions must at times be made, but the rarer the better for peace and harmony. Then, too, it must be remembered that though not the only factor in deciding merit, experience is the most important factor.

When a bill has been referred to the appropriate committee, it is forgotten until somebody, in or out of the committee, presses for its consideration. This automatically disposes of all the bills, and they are by no means few, in which nobody on the ground is particularly interested. Of those that are pressed, the chairman chooses what he pleases for a hearing. Only rarely is his judgment in this matter overthrown by committee vote. His power of suppression is another object of criticism, but as a matter of fact few measures for which there is a really serious demand fail to get a hearing sooner or later.

The busier committees may divide their work among sub-committees, more often with five members than any other number. Some of these might be called standing sub-committees, each handling a certain class of bills. Others are specially selected, each for the bill assigned to it. The sub-committee probably results in more thorough, intelligent study, for, as appears in all the organized activities of men, the more compact the responsibility, the better the work is likely to be done. On the other hand there is the usual concomitant — the smaller the number, the greater the danger of bad judgment. The general experience of mankind with all sorts of small committees is that one man is likely to do about all the work; or in matter of decision is likely to dominate the others. In a Congressional sub-committee the chairman is pretty sure to have preponderating influence, if not to be the absolutely controlling factor. The full committee will, in turn, usually pay great deference to the advice of the sub-committee; and then the House will ordinarily follow the full committee. This, it will be seen, gives one man, the chairman of the sub-committee, an opportunity for influence that may be excessive and dangerous. With the right man, wise, cautious, and yet constructive, the result may be better than could be secured by the friction of many minds in a large committee or in the House itself. On the other hand, sometimes unwise conclusions may be traced to the prejudice, pique, or whim of that one man who dominated a sub-committee. In spite of this element of danger, however, proceeding by use of sub-committees seems unavoidable as long as the work of Congress is so unequally distributed among its committees. Those that are excessively burdened could not begin to handle their tasks if each measure were to be first studied and passed upon in full committee.

Better distribution of committee work is much to be desired. As things go now, so much is asked of a quarter of the members of the House that they cannot do their best, and the capacities of another quarter are not utilized to the most advantage. From the point of view of the individual member, this means that some have a far better chance than others to exert influence and make reputations. Though radical reform would be hard to accomplish, and any close approach to division of responsibilities and opportunities would be impossible, material improvement could and should be made. A step in the right direction was taken when about one sixth of the House committees were designated by the party organizations as "major," with provision that no member assigned to any of these should have any other committee appointment. The result is that more than half the members of the House have but a single committee position. This ought to be carried further with consolidation of minor committees. Any man on more than one committee is exposed to frequent calls to attend two hearings at the same time. The disadvantage of this is worse in the Senate than in the House, for the much smaller membership of the Senate compels far more overlapping of work. Most of the Senators must serve on four or five committees, which is unfortunate. The next step there ought to be reduction of the size of the committees. A large attendance of a small committee is better than a small attendance of a large committee.

Attendance of the public at committee hearings is not prevented, but is not encouraged. As a rule, the only testimony or argument admitted is that coming from persons known to be particularly concerned, or believed to be particularly qualified to inform or advise. If a department or bureau is involved, its head or his representative usually comes upon request, and in that way there is maintained a much closer contact between the legislative and executive branches than is commonly supposed.

Next comes consideration of the bill by the committee in executive session, that is, behind closed doors. This is the most interesting, important, and useful part of the work of a Congressman, and the part of which the public knows nothing. Indeed, the ignorance of the public about it is one of the causes of its usefulness. Behind closed doors nobody can talk to the galleries or the newspaper reporters. Buncombe is not worth while. Only sincerity counts. Men drop their masks. They argue

THE GENESIS OF A STATUTE

to, not through, each other. That is one reason why it would be a calamity if the demand for pitiless publicity of committee deliberations should ever prevail.

Another reason is that publicity would lessen the chance for the concessions, the compromises, without which wise legislation cannot in practice be secured. Men are averse to changing their positions or yielding anything when many eyes are watching. It is in the conference room that agreements are reached, results accomplished.

Furthermore, with privacy it proves possible in most of the committees of Congress for men to work harmoniously in spite of party differences. It is not commonly understood that by far the greater part of the work of Congress is wholly free from partisanship. In the deliberations of no committee on which I have served have I ever heard an argument advanced or seen a vote given from what I had reason to think party considerations, save possibly in the case of one man on one of the committees on Elections, and that in but a single instance. There is only one committee in the House, that on Ways and Means, the revenue-raising committee, which habitually works on party lines. The committee that spends the money, the Committee on Appropriations, usually is unanimous in its reports, and in defending them on the floor its members almost invariably stand shoulder to shoulder, regardless of party.

Critics of Congress would be more generous if they could watch the handling of a long, intricate bill by a committee in executive session. Then they would learn why Congress is doing its most serious work when it seems to be dawdling. After many hours of tedious hearings, they would see many other hours of patient, hard study. They would have to admit the presence of earnestness, sincerity, and patriotism. They would be surprised at the degree of knowledge, intelligence, and common sense displayed. Here comes to the front the man who never makes a speech in the House and whose name never gets into the reports of Congressional doings. Here far more often than on the floor the one vote counts, for it may determine the course of millions of money or affect the interests of millions of men. Twice have I seen this happen. In one instance the amount involved has proved to be nearly $500,000,000. And the public never knew a thing about the episode.

There is no insignificant member of Congress when it comes to votes in committee rooms.

Great gain might follow if the electorate could only be made to understand and appreciate this. There might be a revision of tests to be applied to candidates. The superlative question might be

THE GENESIS OF A STATUTE

made — "Has he the best judgment we can command?" Oratorical power might be discounted. The showy qualities might carry less weight.

If, then, voters would apply the tests to which they are accustomed for the appraisal of judgment in the affairs of daily life, quite different selections might follow. The standards of society in this respect are the result of age-long experience. Men turn to some one of their number for advice or decision or leadership because in his own affairs he has shown himself wiser than his fellows. The test most commonly accepted in our matter-of-fact day is that of success in some occupation calling for enterprise, foresight, prudence, sagacity, common sense. This need not confine the choice of candidates to men who have succeeded in profit-making occupations, for certain types of professional occupation may also demonstrate the same faculties; but it does exclude the man who, from lack of ability or lack of training or lack of experience, has not handled his own affairs with distinct advantage either to himself or to others. In the committee room, where individual judgment may so importantly affect the affairs of this great coöperative agency we call the national government, the well-trained, well-balanced, mature, sound, open mind is above all to be desired. Its possessor can serve his fellow men greatly.

How does it come about that one man can wield so much power in the committee room? It is partly because adverse action by a committee kills a measure, and when opposing views in the committee nearly balance, one man's vote may turn the scale. If he casts it in the affirmative, then the chances all favor finality, for the House will pay little or no attention to the narrowness of the margin and usually will follow the majority. If he casts it in the negative, the House will never have a chance to question the decision.

Adverse action by a committee kills a measure, because, as things now stand, it proves impracticable to get the House to compel a committee to report. Rules to make this possible have proved unworkable. The latest change, that of January, 1924, resulted in but one serious attempt to get a measure away from a reluctant committee, and it failed. There is agreement that there ought to be some practical way to discharge committees in exceptional situations, but nobody has yet been able to suggest how by rule to confine it to such situations, and all recognize the danger in throwing the door wide open to an impatient, impulsive, or cowardly majority.

This power to pigeon-hole, as it is commonly called, that is, to suppress in committee, is one of the fault-finder's grievances. It is, indeed, a dan-

THE GENESIS OF A STATUTE

gerous power, easily susceptible of abuse. Better on the whole is the system of the Massachusetts Legislature, compelling a committee report on every proposal, with opportunity to debate it on the floor of House or Senate. Yet even in Massachusetts, with only about one fifth as many bills introduced annually as in Congress, the need of lessening the strain by giving committees the power to pigeonhole is seriously urged. In Congress, opportunity to discuss every proposal is wholly out of the question. With nearly every one of 435 men anxious of his own accord, or pressed by his constituents, to bring up certain measures, it will be seen that chaos would follow the opportunity. Most of the available time would be used up in considering what to consider.

Even as it is, the struggle for the right of way, for the chance to be heard in the House itself, is no trivial matter. There is not time enough to give consideration to anywhere near all of that small percentage of proposals approved by the committees. So a system of preference is perforce employed It is too intricate to explain here. Suffice it to say that the reports are grouped in what are known as calendars. To some of these are assigned certain days in the week or month, so that part of the bills are likely to be reached almost automatically. These, however, are mostly the less important measures. What may interest us more is the uncertainty about reaching a large part of the really significant proposals.

About forty years ago, when the work of Congress had so grown as to make the need of systematic selection imperative, that responsibility fell into the hands of the Committee on Rules. Extension of its power has been compelled by the steady growth of work, until now it uses practically all the days of the session that are not assigned by the rules to specified classes of business, or occupied by the committees that have special privilege, notably the revenue-raising and money-spending committees. In practice the result is that only two classes of business have a reasonable chance for what might be called automatic consideration,— the extremes: the most important, for the wheels of government must be kept moving; and the least important, the measures to which there is no serious objection, which come up by unanimous consent, or under certain conditions with less than three objectors. From the mass of measures in between the extremes, the Committee on Rules makes selection.

In 1909 these conditions had become so intolerable that Wednesday of each week was set aside for a call of committees, so that each in its turn might, in each of two successive weeks, bring up such of its reports as it might see fit to select. The relief has

THE GENESIS OF A STATUTE

proved quite inadequate. In the 68th Congress (1923-1925) less than one third of the committees were reached, and so had the chance that the rule contemplated. This in part may explain why so much work was left unfinished when Congress adjourned.

The worst of it is that in the unfinished work are most of the proposals for improvement in the processes of government. These are the things that can wait, and so are deferred. Time and outgrown parliamentary methods permit handling little more than the picayune and the insistent things.

Suppose, however, that the bill whose career we are following is one of the lucky measures to be reached for debate. Here comes in play for the first time the general parliamentary law, as modified by the practices peculiar to Congress, found in its rules and precedents. The resultant system is unique. The member fresh from some state legislature finds himself bewildered and helpless. Only by years of absorbing will he arrive at understanding the reasons and mastering the intricacies. As a matter of fact, however, it all has surprisingly little effect on the form of the great bulk of legislation. It may defeat, delay, or expedite; it may now and then result in some amendments of much consequence; but most of the bills that go through House and Senate are not seriously changed.

The popular conception of the floor-work of Congress is quite wrong. Most of the talking has no effect on legislation. That in the Senate has more or less of useful effect in shaping public opinion, for it gets a little attention in the press. That in the House has almost none of even this utility, for the work of the House is nowadays ignored by the press, save on the rarest occasions.

The day of the old-time parliamentary orator has passed. Few of the members of the House will stay on the floor to listen to long speeches. As the newspapers will rarely print even as much as a brief abstract, and the only readers will be those few who peruse the Congressional Record or the pamphlets sent out by members to their constituents, the incentive for laborious preparation and exhaustive discussion is small. Leave to revise and extend remarks in the Record gives almost the only opportunity to marshal facts and set forth opinion in a well-balanced argument. The rules and the conditions virtually preclude thorough treatment of any one subject by any one speaker in the House itself. Nominally, there may be speeches an hour long, but he is a lucky man who ever gets more than half an hour, and most of the speeches presumed to be addressed to the principles of a measure must be compressed into from ten to twenty minutes, which is, of course, too short for any comprehensive treatment.

THE GENESIS OF A STATUTE

This comes about through the practice now almost invariable of determining in advance the total amount of time to be consumed in the debate on the bill as a whole. When the Committee on Rules brings in its special rule for the consideration of a certain bill, as it does in the case of nearly all the important measures other than the appropriation bills, the rule usually specifies the time that may be used in what is called "general debate," which need not be confined to the subject matter of the bill unless the rule so specifies. Ordinarily half of the time is to be controlled by the chairman of the committee concerned and half by the senior member (the ranking member) of the committee who opposes. Thereupon men who want to speak go to those who thus get control of the time, and ask for ten, fifteen, or such other number of minutes as they see fit to name. Of course the dispensers of the precious minutes want to satisfy as many of their allies as possible, and when the requests are numerous, as is frequently the case, the fractions of the total are likely to be small. Members of the committee concerned get the preference, and it not infrequently happens that they use up all the time, leaving no opportunity whatever for anybody else to share in the general discussion.

In this matter, as indeed in most others, the House lacks the sense of proportion. The allotment of time for the consideration of the various measures bears little relation to their relative importance. Measures in which the public takes a keen and vital interest, on which fifty or a hundred members would like to speak, are often allotted no more than two or three times as many hours as other measures of but a tenth or twentieth as much importance. Some of the biggest things are put through by use of the motion to suspend the rules, which permits but forty minutes of discussion all told.

All this is unfortunate, for it precludes a great deal of the help that might be given by well-informed men, capable of effective argument; but the pressure of work probably makes adequate remedy out of the question. The most that can be hoped under present conditions is that the Committee on Rules may be persuaded to pay more attention to the relative importance of the measures making up the business of the House, and to insist that the big things shall have more time, getting it by forcing the summary disposal of the little things.

The most interesting and useful discussion is that under the five-minute rule, when the House in Committee of the Whole is considering a bill section by section for amendment. The debate then is more informal; it is likely to be conversational rather than oratorical; argument must perforce be concise and to the point; decisions quickly follow.

THE GENESIS OF A STATUTE 23

The comparative unimportance and inefficacy of most of the proceedings on the floor of the House furnish one cause of the small attendance that so surprises and disturbs chance visitors in the gallery. As a matter of fact, the absentees are for the most part in their offices, busy with the manifold duties brought to a Congressman by his relations with his constituents. If a vote seems to anybody to require the presence of a quorum, the call-bells will be rung and the absentees will come trooping over from the office building. This has one serious consequence. The issue is likely to be determined by men who have not heard a word of the argument. No real harm follows in the many instances where the question is more or less familiar and men have already made up their minds; but just the same it discredits the value of debate. To be sure, debate in the House rarely changes votes, but not to have a fair chance to try to convince or persuade is discouraging.

Results especially regrettable follow when measures more or less technical come along. For instance, whenever the Committee on Banking and Currency gets the right of way, the attendance dwindles rapidly. Most of the members know little and care less about banking problems. They are quite content to "follow the committee." This makes it almost useless for a committee member who may not chance to agree with the majority of his fellow committeemen, to try to upset their report on the floor. No matter how convincing his argument, it will be in vain, because it will not reach the ears of the greater part of the men who will vote.

Were it not for this aspect of the voting methods, a small attendance would be a gain rather than a loss. The House does its best work with from fifty to a hundred members on the floor. There is less confusion, more attention, and better use of time. The men acquainted with both sides of the particular question at issue are likely to be on hand. On the whole, when the decision is confined to them, it is apt to be wiser than it would be if four times as many members were there.

In the Senate the discursive and voluminous character of debate has for many years been the cause of sharp criticism. It has undoubtedly wasted a great deal of precious time. Used for filibustering purposes, to prevent action, it has received showers of obloquy. Yet the question is not so one-sided as the public thinks. Many of the wise men who have served in the Senate have come to believe — for often they have changed their minds after long experience — that it is important that there should be one place in the legislative journey where the opportunity for discussion is unfettered. They have found that this has not in the end prevented any decision persistently wanted by the people, but on the other hand has stood in the way of much action that the country has come to conclude would have been unwise.

By far the larger number of the Senators are not, as individual members, at fault. They are industrious men, much overworked. They do not neglect the public business, nor are they indifferent to the public welfare. But they are at the mercy of a few voluble colleagues who lamentably waste the hours in vain speech.

The remedy is not evident. Time limits in the Senate would be in many ways unfortunate. Adequately thorough discussion of public questions being no longer practicable in the House, there ought to be left opportunity for it in the Senate. Otherwise the public would not be informed at all as to the merits and demerits of a large part of the proposals for the better conduct of its affairs. How to secure proper discussion and at the same time to suppress the demagogue and the bore, nobody has yet made clear. Perhaps the only remedy will be to persuade the states not to send demagogues or bores to the Senate.

Drastic extension of the meagre form of closure that the Senate reluctantly accepted not long ago, may not be the best remedy for the bad phases of the present situation. At any rate, prudence might advise trying first the enforcement of a familiar rule of parliamentary law that the Senate constantly ignores. One of the prime requirements as to speech in any well-regulated assembly is that it shall be addressed to the subject in hand — in other words be pertinent, relevant, germane. Were the Senate to profit in this particular by the experience and example of nearly all the other legislative bodies of the world, not only would filibustering be made much harder, but also the ordinary work of the Senate would be handled with far more expedition.

In general the parliamentary practice of Congress works equitably, and in many respects effectively. It has, however, one serious weakness in common with the practice of most other legislative assemblies, and that is in the matter of amendments. These are often drafted on the spur of the moment, without time for due study of either substance or form. Inasmuch as resort to any second stage for further amendment is thought impracticable, the result is that bills may be, and sometimes are, badly damaged. Fortunately the danger is partly met by the possibility of correction in the other branch, or in the conference committee that turns out to be usually required for reconciling differences between the branches; but the practice is not so workmanlike and prudent as that which prevails, for instance, in the Massachusetts Legislature, with two stages for

THE GENESIS OF A STATUTE

amendment and the advice of a revising committee between, in each branch.

In some other details of this sort there could be improvement, but the really important criticism is to be fairly aimed at the system as a whole in its relation to the volume of work now to be handled. Shaped for the most part in simpler days, when the volume of business was small, much of the practice is now archaic and outgrown. Tenacious adherence to processes for which the reason long ago disappeared makes it the despair of men who value the minutes and who vainly bemoan the waste of time. For example, Congress continues oral reading in full by a reading clerk — a practice that was necessary in Parliament centuries past, because so many of its members could not read the bills. In the body where it began, it was long ago abandoned, the reliance being placed instead on printed copies. Such a tiresome, useless waste of time as it entails is likewise no longer endured in the best of our state legislatures; but it persists in Congress, with the result of throwing away nearly if not quite a month of every term in mere clerical enunciation.

From a month to six weeks more of every term is wasted in quorum calls. Each of those in the House takes nearly half an hour, and three or four hundred times in the course of a Congress the bells may be set ringing at the demand of some one member.

The pretence of reading the Journal, to which nobody listens, adds a few minutes each day to the total of waste. The toleration of irrelevant debate is a more serious matter, using to no good end a great many hours. Another waste comes from the protracted discussion of points of order. These and other habits no longer endured in the best-regulated legislative assemblies of the world sacrifice, needlessly, at least a quarter of the time in every session.

Nothing but inertia prevents palpable remedy. Were it not for this inertia, Congressmen might easily have the Saturday holiday that gives members of Parliament so much relief. Or it might adjourn an hour earlier each afternoon, with that much more of chance for life-prolonging recreation. Or it might sit two or three months less in every term. Or it might satisfy a complaining people with a third more of achievement.

Let it not be supposed that in our day the House has made no progress whatever in saving time. To its credit should be put one distinct achievement found in greatly lessening the waste due to filibustering. The public is hardly yet aware that filibustering has almost disappeared from the lower branch. Not more than once or twice in a session has there been of late years any serious resort to this device, or anything like the protracted battles that were frequent a generation ago. The changes in the rules

THE GENESIS OF A STATUTE

brought about through the leadership of Speaker Reed, under circumstances with an element of the dramatic that aroused the public interest, were long ago accepted as wise by everybody. By interpretation and by the development of a body of precedent under them, the practice has been so shaped that it is now recognized as well-nigh hopeless to try to filibuster. The game is to-day rarely worth the candle. The solitary obstructionist has only one really important weapon left. He can still exercise the privilege deduced from the constitutional requirement as to the presence of a quorum; for the theory is that any one man may at any time call attention to a violation of the Constitution and compel its observance. If the obstructionists are numerous enough, they can bring into play another constitutional requirement, that for a vote by Yeas and Nays on the demand of one fifth of the members present. As each roll-call takes nearly half an hour, a determined minority can still waste much time, and occasionally it will even now force the laying aside of a measure; but as a rule in these days a majority gets its way with reasonable expedition.

Possibly this is in some degree due to the wane in party spirit of late years. Since the World War the lower branch of Congress has not been the scene of much political strife. That has been left to the

Senate, where oratory is unchecked and the filibuster is an easy resort. The rules of the Senate are not so stringent and efficacious as those of the House. Indeed, new Senators fresh from the House are likely to declare in disgust that the Senate has no rules. Whether for this reason or some other, or a combination of reasons, conditions in the Senate still invite partisanship and give it full scope. Those who believe in party government of the extreme type will see in this an advantage, but even they must admit the damage in the corollary — lamentable waste of time and costly failure to get the public business transacted.

Returning to the bill we are following, we find that, after it has run the gauntlet of one branch, it has to go through the same process in the other. Whether or not the two-chamber or bicameral system is the better, and regardless of the fact that it is disappearing from city governments and is on the defensive in the states, the chance of any change in the Federal framework is so remote as to make discussion of that system in connection with Congress purely academic. Attention may be called, however, to the fact that its operation has some defects which might be cured. Experience in some of the state legislatures has shown beyond question that the joint committee system has important advantages not to be found in the separately working commit-

ures fail because they have not been considered in both branches. The Senate is the chief sinner. Of late years the House has far surpassed the Senate in carrying its work through to a conclusion. The public, however, exercising no discrimination, views the work of Congress as a whole, and so in its blame treats the lower branch most unfairly.

When at last our typical bill has passed both branches and been signed by the President, or passed over his veto, a statute has been born after great travail. It finds itself one of a small band of survivors, barely three per cent of the number of the measures introduced. To be sure, many bills, such as those for pensions, have been consolidated into a few measures; but leaving them out of account, it will be found that not one proposal in twenty has reached enactment. Of those that survive, a large proportion consists of private bills and of trivial adjustments in the machinery of government. The really consequential enactments of Congress are few. Yet it is forced to share in the indiscriminate condemnation nowadays visited on all law-making bodies because of the volume of current legislation. The truth is that the sins of Congress are far more those of omission than of commission. It does not meet the expectations of the people. The remedy is largely within its own control.

tees of the two branches of Congress. The loss of time by two committee considerations is evident, and not offset by the fact that a bill which fails to pass one House need not be considered by a committee of the other. Furthermore, the joint committee makes gain by reconciling many differences, particularly in matters of detail, before report is made, thus saving much loss of effort when compared with the Congressional method of harmonizing views in conference committee after the bill has passed each branch.

The joint committee brings a benefit less tangible, yet of no small consequence, in establishing personal contacts between Senators and Representatives, with the benefits that come from acquaintance and mutual understanding. At present Senators and Representatives see little and know little of each other either inside or outside the Capitol. This does not conduce to harmonious coöperation for the public welfare.

The lack of this coöperation is the most serious defect in the machinery of Congress. More than any other one thing it gives ground for public grievance. The fault is not that one House may differ in judgment from the other. That is one of the virtues of the bicameral system. The trouble is that one House may not pass at all upon the judgment of the other. Every term sees important meas-

Lecture II

LAWS AND EXCEPTIONS

ALARM prevails in certain quarters over the growth of lawmaking. Legislators are said to be too much controlling the individual, to be harassing him, and to be interfering with sundry inherent rights. To determine whether there is ground for apprehension, it is necessary first to know something about law, its nature and its scope.

Such law as concerns us here is that which systematically impels conduct.

Reflect on that definition and you will see that it includes impulsions that come from some authority outside mankind, or from the pressures of the social relations, or from some definite human authority.

Divinity as the source of law was once the well-nigh universal conception, and is still accepted by many millions of men. In Germany it was stoutly urged by the last Emperor, and apparently believed by his people. However, with the wrecking of monarchies by the World War, it may be said that on three of the world's continents it is no longer a widespread belief that governmental institutions are based on divine will, at least in any definite way.

Yet there persists, even in the United States, a theory that there is a Law of Nature superior to any human enactment and controlling where the two conflict. This theory is put forward notably at the moment by those who deny any binding force in the Eighteenth Amendment to the Constitution of the United States (known as the Prohibition Amendment), as well as by some who argue against the adoption of the child-labor amendment and who object to not a few of the social measures pressed upon our lawmaking assemblies. The contention must be met by any lawmaker who would defend the validity and supremacy of such legislation in which he has shared.

To appreciate that the issue is fundamental, recall that not only was it at the core of the Civil War, but also that it furnished to the American colonies the ground for defying acts of Parliament and was placed in the very forefront of the Declaration of Independence, which was the cornerstone of our country. The founders declared that all men are endowed by their Creator with certain unalienable rights; that among these are Life, Liberty, and the Pursuit of Happiness. Is that declaration to be accepted literally, or is it subject to so much construction and so many exceptions as to have little or no vitality in its application to present-day problems of legislation?

LAWS AND EXCEPTIONS 35

In seeking an answer to this question, first observe that under all governments both life and liberty have always been held to be subject to the sovereign power. Each must be sacrificed if the common welfare demands. Military service with its contingency of death has ever been a necessary adjunct of statehood. Full liberty of action is unthinkable in organized society. Happiness may not be pursued an inch beyond the bounds of another's personality or property. Clearly, then, if natural right exists, it is only within limitations.

If there are limits, who sets them, man or Nature? Are they the same, yesterday, to-day, and forever? Or do they change with time and circumstance?

These queries suggest the endless casuistry that the subject invites. Pedants have been splitting hairs over it for centuries. Yet practical men may think that for practical purposes a few rather simple considerations will suffice. They start with the presumption that the existence of a state means organization for the common benefit. The problem then is to determine what is for the common benefit. The greatest good of the greatest number will be the test. Of the two factors the greatest number is the easier to recognize and determine. Palpably, if the majority does not prevail, the minority will. If the majority may not prevent the sale of lottery tickets, habit-forming drugs, alcoholic beverages, then the opinions of the minority will prevail, which is inconsistent with the principle of a democratic state.

What may be the greatest good, is harder to decide. Nothing better for the purpose than the machinery of representative government has yet been devised. It starts with the presumption that the will of the majority is most likely to secure the greatest good. Always, however, we must bear in mind that injury to the minority, even if it be but one man, may contain such menace to the ultimate good of the majority as to overcome the prospect of immediate benefit. An illustration may make this clear. Suppose the greatest good of the greatest number requires taking a man's land for a street. Two questions arise: Is the immediate convenience of the public more important than the ultimate harm from depriving men of their property against their will? Is the gain to the taxpayers if no payment is made, likely to offset the loss that may come through the shrinkage of all land values from the knowledge that anybody's land may at any time be taken from him without compensation? Each question, it will be seen, requires that the ultimate as well as the immediate good shall be considered.

This does not concede any rights to the individual by reason of his personality, but it does concede that what he looks on as natural, inherent,

LAWS AND EXCEPTIONS

unalienable rights may be conditions which it is for the advantage of the state itself to preserve and protect. It may also be conceded that there are some rights which are more precious than others to the individual, and which the state should be more solicitous about infringing. These are the rights that men have come to speak of as natural and unalienable. Perhaps the quarrel is largely one of phraseology. In any case, it seems clear that as a matter of fact there is no right which the state does not at times invade. In this it always has insisted and always will insist upon the supremacy of its own judgment. What rights it is most to the ultimate advantage of the state to preserve and protect, what rights the individual shall last be called upon to yield, is for the state and not for the individual to determine. Into the controversy as to whether the state should make this determination through its legislative or its judicial branch, or whether they may well share in that function, we need not here enter. The present occasion will be met if it is shown that at any rate the determination is not beyond the legislative power. Surely that will not be denied if it is admitted that the common welfare is the very purpose of legislation.

Rejecting, then, the notion that the individual has any rights the state is bound to respect regardless of its own real and ultimate advantage, in other words, that there is any such thing as a paramount Natural Law of independent existence, turn next to that class of law which signifies the impulsion of social pressures. Mostly it is unwritten law. We call much of it customs, fashions, habits, manners. It may be conveniently classified into laws of the person and laws of property.

We engage in learning the laws of personal conduct from the first conscious moment of our existence. Childhood is one continuous lesson in them. The "dos" and "don'ts" of the home are the necessary repetition of some. Others are taught on the playground and in the school and in the church. Their volume is enormous. They concern every phase of the personal contact between human beings. They govern almost every active moment of our waking hours.

Part of them are mere conventions, devoid of any element of reason, agreed upon as devices for saving time, effort, and confusion — such, for example, as the rule that men meeting on the sidewalk shall pass to the right. Others began, and sometimes continue, with a reason — such as the rule that food shall be carried to the mouth with a fork, as less dangerous than a knife. Time was, however, when the rule was the reverse, forks having only two tines and being so much less convenient than knives that their disadvantage more than offset the danger of

LAWS AND EXCEPTIONS

the knifeblade. This may suggest why from time to time unwritten laws of daily life may change.

Some, however, embody principles more enduring and far more important. Chief among them are those constituting what we ordinarily mean by "morality." To illustrate, consider truth and falsehood. Did you ever reflect how gravely inconvenient it would be if in our daily relations with our fellows truth were not the normal thing and could not be confidently expected? Imagine your embarrassment if to every question you ask, little or big, there would be nothing unnatural in a false reply. So habitually do we tell the truth, that we never think of its value in countless circumstances. There are countries where it is not enforced by custom, but, in part because thereof, they are what we call backward and uncivilized. In our own country there are individuals who often refuse to employ it, and thereby make mischief. Yet so nearly adequate for control are the social pressures that falsehood as such is forbidden by no written law. Only when it is told under oath, and becomes perjury, have we put it under an enacted ban.

Indeed there are comparatively few of the myriad rules governing personal relations that we have found it necessary to set forth in statutes. With those relating to property the case is otherwise. The pressure of opinion has not sufficed to protect the fruits of the labor of men, and at every turn safety has to be sought at the hands of government. Note, however, that even in this matter a great deal is left to the force of custom, become almost instinctive in the greater part of mankind. Not primarily because we are afraid of policemen do most of us keep our hands off the property of others. It is because of our respect for the opinions of others and for ourselves.

From these considerations it should be apparent that the function of legislators is to bring the help of written law to the aid of public opinion for the better enforcement of preëxistent rules. This help is chiefly to be given by adding the machinery of government — police officers, courts, fines, or confinement — to the impelling forces of society that have not been found adequate.

If that be true, then, except as legislative bodies fashion new penalties, they do not make new law, save where no custom has arisen, no opinion has been crystallized, as, for example, in the present situation regarding radio, or that of aircraft. Even with the novel problems, however, those now created so frequently by science, invention, and industrial development, the initial solutions are usually worked out by the social forces themselves rather than by their incidental device known as government.

LAWS AND EXCEPTIONS

What takes place may be shown by the automobile as clearly as by anything else.

While automobiles were few and slow, they called for no new law. Presently reckless drivers ignored the general judgment as to what was safe, and rushed through cities and towns regardless of danger. Municipal ordinances, which are local statutes, became necessary to regulate speed. Evils growing, the state legislatures had to provide registration and licensing systems, rules and penalties. Now the truck and the motor bus, with their interstate traffic, have brought us to the place where Congress must take a hand. Meanwhile, the increase in the number of cars and the putting of many of them in the control of men morally, mentally, or physically unqualified for such responsibility have so increased the menace to human life, fatal accidents have become so numerous, that the complete inadequacy of social control is clear and more of legal control is everywhere demanded. Especially significant is the action of the public mind in the matter of drunken drivers. Here if anywhere it would be expected that common opinion would suffice. Everybody knows the folly of driving a car after taking a drink. To paraphrase the famous French *mot* about the execution of the Duc d'Enghien, the man who does it is worse than a criminal, he is a fool, and fools ought not to be allowed to endanger our lives. Yet the universal judgment in this matter has not been able to deter the man with no self-respect and no care for others. So we must put him where for a time he cannot slaughter his fellow men, our hope being that this may lead him to sanity.

The use of liquor in general furnishes one of the most instructive instances of the way statutes come about. The need of some regulation of the liquor traffic by law appeared in the earliest days of the American colonies. For the most part, however, this was left to the individual and social conscience till the last century. With the factory era came more and more of widespread injury from the traffic. The total abstinence movement and the preaching of temperance, useful though they were, did not seem to the majority of the people in many localities to be meeting the need. So resort to written law was demanded and secured. The purely economic forces came to the help of the movement, finally winning national prohibition. It is sheer nonsense to say that Congress or the state legislatures forced this on the people. What the Senators and Representatives did was to enact into law, constitutional and statutory, the evident wishes of the majority of the citizens in the greater part of their constituencies.

The same sort of thing had taken place in the case of other conspicuous social injuries. A century or so ago the public awoke to the useless and foolish waste of human life by the practice of dueling. The death of Alexander Hamilton at the hands of Aaron Burr had emphasized the fact that the loss was often of the most valuable human lives. Public opinion unaided could not end the folly, so it summoned law to its help. Provisions against dueling were put in the Constitutions of twenty-eight states, and doubtless everywhere else in the land it would to-day be treated as a crime.

Much the same is the history of the laws against gambling, lotteries, habit-forming drugs, food adulterations, and a long list of practices dangerous to happiness, health, and life. Every one of them was enacted for the protection of society against an evil it could not sufficiently handle by its own pressures, without the help of the penalties that accompany formulated and authoritative prohibitions.

Observe that the enactment implies a hope and not an assurance. There are those who contend that no law should be put on the statute book unless it can be enforced. Inasmuch as there is no statute that is everywhere and always enforced, evidently the question is one of degree and the contention might be ruled out on the ground of uncertainty; but assuming that reasonable enforcement is meant and that we could agree as to what is reasonably to be expected, does it follow that the demand is pertinent? Who would apply the test to one of the unwritten laws of our social relations? For example, should there be no rules of grammar because many persons speak ungrammatically? Should there be no fashions because many persons are unfashionable? Should idleness be condoned because many persons are lazy, or insolence because many are saucy, or waste because spendthrifts are plenty? And when society decides to call in the help of its agency known as government to secure greater compliance with its wishes, shall it be debarred or even deterred because even then its wishes may be largely thwarted? Of course enforcement is to be desired, non-enforcement is unfortunate and to be deplored, but neither is a legitimate factor in determining the propriety or expediency of law. The real question is whether a preëxistent purpose can be helped by solemn declaration in statutory form.

Note that the purpose is not novel. Yet it is said again and again that Congress and the legislatures are of their own initiative trying to make men good by law. We at whose doors the responsibility is thus laid are charged with being bigots and fanatics. We are called busybodies who interfere with the private affairs of the citizen. What have we really done? In accordance with the assumptions and presumptions of the representative form of government, we have represented our constituencies in deciding whether this or that evil was beyond the control of social pressures and required the supplementing of those pressures with the prohibitions and penalties of statutes. We have initiated nothing.

Furthermore, we have invaded no personal liberty that had not already been invaded. We have declared nothing wrong that had not already been declared wrong by a myriad tongues. Their concurrence had created a rule of conduct that had secured widespread compliance through what we call moral compulsion. It was a rule with penalties that may have ranged from criticism to obloquy, or from loss of income to loss of friendship, good-will, respect — penalties sometimes more bitter than any that courts ever impose. Yet nobody questioned the right of society to make such a rule; nobody said it transgressed any individual perquisite. Doubtless some complied with it unwillingly, ungraciously, resentfully, but they did not doubt its legitimacy. Others may have disputed, evaded, scorned, but not on the ground that the rule deprived them of inherent rights. That is not the test applied to customs, fashions, manners, "mores" — the unwritten law. Men disobey this or that unwritten canon because they want to, not because it runs counter to some inherent privilege, natural or supernatural. To much the greater part of the social code, however, all men conform. By compliance with it in every hour of their conscious lives, they admit that it is not invalid simply because it restricts personal freedom. Why, then, should they flame into indignant revolt against the outrage upon their individuality when the majority of their fellows decide that another one of the rules of conduct constituting the code of society shall be promulgated with the formalities and subject to the consequences of enacted law?

All this, it will be seen, makes public opinion the source of legislation, and therein is but repeating the views of Rousseau, Bryce, and many another expounder of political science. It is not true, however, that the legislator plays or should play no constructive part. He must lead as well as follow. The paradox is explained if you consider that public opinion is often vague, unformed, perhaps hardly more than an instinct. The legislator has the duty of enlightening and guiding, forming and formulating. This it is that justifies him in constructive thought. Were it otherwise, he need never concern himself with more than trying to determine what people want. Limited to a matter of interpretation, the task would never attract men of originality and genius. The race of statesmen would disappear. It will be a sad day when representatives are forbidden to think of what the people ought to want, a sad day when leadership becomes an offence. A citizen

LAWS AND EXCEPTIONS

does not cease to be a citizen upon election to office. Because he is placed where it is his duty, and where he has the opportunity, to learn more, to study more, and to reflect more, his obligation to inform, to suggest, to advise, and to lead, is all the greater. Therefore law itself may and should help build public opinion.

This does not mean that the lawmaker of to-day is akin to the lawgivers of olden time. He is not to play the part of a Solon or Lycurgus. His opportunities and obligations are not even those of the so-called absolute monarchs of more recent centuries, men who affected to despise or ignore public opinion, though even they could not keep their thrones if they long outraged the views of those immediately about them or the warriors upon whom they depended for support. Fiat law is no longer tolerated. Men have come generally to agree that where the will of the majority is definite and clear, it is to prevail; and where it is indefinite and vague, it must be assumed to be in harmony with the general mass of customs and mental habits. In other words, law must accord with the common sense of the people. Subject to this limitation, the judgment of the legislator may have full scope. If he errs in construing the temper of the people, if he misconceives their needs, his law will not survive. There can be no successful government unless in the end law and public opinion agree.

Furthermore, grave responsibilities are imposed upon the legislator by the fact that the public rarely has any useful opinion in matter of detail. Men may be clear as to purpose without ever giving serious thought to the machinery for accomplishing that purpose. For example, they may object to the use of money in elections, or to the delivery of fireproof coal for furnaces, or to the importation of crop-destroying insects, or to the monopolization of water-power, and yet not have anything like agreement as to how to stop these things. This, you will see, greatly limits the part public opinion plays in legislation, and correspondingly increases that of the legislator. As a matter of fact, it is easily possible to over-emphasize the public opinion phase of legislative work. However, when it does come to the front, it brings to the lawmaker some of his hardest problems and also attracts naturally the most attention from the public, so that it should be further examined.

The most difficult task that confronts the legislator is to find out what may be the preponderance of public opinion on any given topic. I am inclined to think that the harder he works to find this out, the less he accomplishes. At every turn of his activity he invites deception.

He can safely put reliance on no popular vote. Napoleon was not wide of the mark in declaring:

LAWS AND EXCEPTIONS

"The first duty of a prince is doubtless to do that which a people wants; but that which a people wants is hardly ever that which it says." Who that has heard a group of ordinarily intelligent men confess how they voted on a number of referenda, and why, can doubt the truth of this? Lack of information is the predominant and sufficient cause. Rare, very rare, is the voter who has acquainted himself with all the facts and who has read or heard thorough argument from both sides. Few, very few, are the men and women who study public questions and who reflect upon what they learn. Most persons have not the leisure, the patience, the training, or the inclination for such tasks. How can it be expected that, when many thousands of the uninformed engage in a plebiscite on other than a few simple questions of broad policy, much weight can be safely attached to the verdict?

Petitions are even more untrustworthy. In the secrecy of the polling booth the voter will exercise his own judgment, if he has any, but when with many others he signs a petition, there is no warrantable presumption that he knows what he is asking or expresses his own view. So many men sign petitions because they are asked and for one reason or another do not want to refuse, that no experienced legislator will dare to put trust in them. That is the reason why they are treated so cavalierly in every legislative body. Congressmen present them out of courtesy and they are listed in the Congressional Record, but their titles are no longer read aloud in the House, and as soon as they reach the committees to which they are referred, they disappear. I have never known a petition to be laid before a committee in session. The brutal fact then is that petitions have no direct effect on legislation. Indirectly they doubtless have some value through acquainting part of the signers with the existence of an agitation for this or that purpose, getting them to think about it, and perhaps enlisting them in that active spread of ideas which finally embodies public opinion in law.

Almost as futile so far as direct effect on Congress is concerned, are the resolutions of state legislatures. Your Congressman is likely to think that he knows as much about the subject involved as the men who voted on the question in the legislature; if it is a national question, it is his duty to know more. Often he has sat in a legislature and well understands how little real thought is there given to resolutions of this character. Those who vote for them risk nothing and may gain favor with somebody. Their votes cannot be safely assumed to reflect the genuine opinion of a majority of their constituents. On the other hand, they invite a real harm, for they give a spineless Congressman the chance to excuse himself

LAWS AND EXCEPTIONS 51

by saying he voted this way or that because his state legislature told him so to do.

Resolutions adopted by organizations and associations of all kinds are more substantial, for one may be reasonably confident that as a rule they were not instigated from outside and do convey the real judgment of those who with understanding approved them. When they have been the subject of earnest, informed discussion, they count; but the trouble is that the perfunctory factor is large, and that even where there has been argument, it may have been one-sided, with the decision reached through the influence of zealots.

The printed arguments with which every member of Congress is bombarded — the things we lump under the name of propaganda and with which we surcharge our waste-baskets — rarely show that the authors or signers have studied both sides of the question or have given any thought to contingent considerations. On the other hand, they often do show prejudice, misinformation, or sheer ignorance. Furthermore, they are but fragmentary evidences. The vast and silent majority may feel just the other way.

The newspapers are more helpful. Editorials are the studied work of men more or less informed, who have had some training in the ascertainment and interpretation of the popular mind. It is their business to gather the raw material of public opinion, manufacture it, and sell the product to a public willing to pay for seeing its own ideas in print — sometimes, to be sure, ideas the readers never knew they had, but the ownership of which they will not disavow. Yet editors are no more nearly infallible than Congressmen, and though they help, they do not suffice.

Where, then, shall the lawmaker turn to know what the public really wants? Nowhere, and yet everywhere. If he but talks and listens and reads, a thousand influences will gradually mould his judgment, and presently he will find himself voting as the greater part of his constituents would vote if they had the information and were in his place.

That to my mind is the essence of true representative government. The lawmaker is not to be purely an agent, vainly trying to decide what the majority of his principals desire. He is not to be purely a trustee, making wholly independent decisions, self-conceived and self-sustained. He is to be both agent and trustee as far as may be. He is to feel it as much his duty to try to modify in others opinions with which he disagrees, as to try to let his own opinions be modified by the advice of others. He is to deal fairly both by his constituents and by himself. Such a man deems it necessary to break with constituency or with party only on those very rare occasions when

LAWS AND EXCEPTIONS

Judgment must step aside and let Conscience rule. The great mass of legislation is matter of expediency. Not once in a thousand times is it matter of what is usually thought of as right and wrong. Only when right and wrong are at stake may the legislator refuse to concede, to compromise, or to yield.

More frequent is the problem when public opinion is in error. Public opinion is not infallible. For this reason it is persuasive, but not compelling. Men in the mass are at times prejudiced, angry, impulsive, unjust. So at times the legislator must stand up against prejudice and passion, impulse and injustice. If resistance to opinion when it is wrong proves unavailing, the legislator should yield his office rather than his judgment. Nothing short of that will bring him peace of mind.

Still another problem of the legislator must not be overlooked. He may be well aware that public opinion frowns on some course of conduct, and yet he may, indeed he must, ask himself if the social pressures cannot meet the occasion without the help of written law. Here, you see, is matter of difficult and delicate judgment. It often puts the conscientious lawmaker in a dilemma. He may feel that a statute is not yet necessary, but if he so votes, he may be charged with lack of sympathy with the end in view, while the truth is that he is its warm friend. Do not chide him overmuch if under such circumstances he is slow to act. I venture the belief that the greater part of the members of Congress dislike legislation. Their impulse is to say "No" rather than "Yes." They have to be argued or somehow driven into affirmative action. This the critics do not understand and the public is slow to believe. Yet it accounts in part for the delays and the refusals blamed by half the country. At the same time, the other half is scolding because there are so many new laws. Is there nobody to give Congress credit for the things it does not do?

Even where the need for legislation is apparent, under our dual form of government it has to be decided whether action should be taken by Congress or by the state legislatures. Possibly action is not permitted to Congress by the Constitution. Many citizens fail to understand that Congress is thus restricted. Where either state or nation may act, Congress refuses much more often than the critics suppose. Service in Washington stiffens in most men the hostility to centralized government. When a vote seems to belie this, it is pretty sure to be defended as a justifiable exception to what is agreed should be the rule. Watching the machinery of Federal government at close range satisfies most observers that the fathers did wisely in planning to leave the great bulk of governmental responsibility

LAWS AND EXCEPTIONS

to the states. Actual dealing with the departments and bureaus such as every Congressman must constantly engage in, teaches him that it is better for the citizen just as far as practicable to rely on agencies near-by, more easily reached, more efficiently supervised, more sympathetically responsive to local conditions and needs. So far as centralization gains, it is because of economic or social pressures that are irresistible, and not because of eager approval on the part of Senators and Representatives.

Public opinion ought to have, and in fact does have, very little to do with one class of statutes constituting more than half the enactments by the legislative bodies of the land. That is the class of what is known as private or special legislation. Properly speaking, it is not made up of laws, but of exceptions to laws. Whether it be to redress some individual grievance or to grant some particular privilege, the enactment in question takes place because otherwise the end in view could not be accomplished without violating some general law unless the general law were changed, and such change is either impracticable or thought to be undesirable. Inasmuch, then, as no one exception to a general law or the general body of laws is likely to arouse a general opinion, these matters are for the most part left to the discretion of the legislator. To be sure, the public may approve or oppose a class of these exceptions, as in the case of pensions or charters of one kind or another, but so seldom does this contingency arise that it may here be left out of account.

Originally these enactments were almost all in the way of redress of individual grievances, and were made by assemblies because with the legislative they combined the judicial power. They were courts of last resort, or administered equity. They are still in effect equity courts in so far as they furnish remedies not to be had in the law courts. Nowadays, however, it is almost never equity as between individuals, that field having been turned over to the courts. It is now equity as between the citizen and the state that burdens the legislators. Perhaps half the states of the Union have advanced far enough to permit themselves to be sued. The other half still hold that "the King can do no wrong," and persist in requiring the citizen they have injured to crave for mercy rather than to demand justice. The nation began to yield seventy years ago by establishing a Court of Claims. At first this tribunal had power to do no more than investigate and recommend. From time to time its functions have been enlarged, but Congress loosens its grip on work most reluctantly and still insists on handling a grievously large part of this particular kind. Presently common sense will win, but not so much because it is common sense, as because lack of time will drive Congress to

LAWS AND EXCEPTIONS

send this part of its business where it ought to have been sent long ago — to judicial bodies with equity powers.

For the same reason it will be driven to turn over to existing or newly created agencies a great part of the other demands for special or private legislation it now tries to handle. In the aggregate this work makes a serious inroad on its time. Of the measures enacted by the last four Congresses, about one quarter are classified as private bills or resolutions. The classification does not show the full extent of the mischief. By statute Congress has so restricted the application of the word "private" that many bills really special in nature are classified as "public." As a matter of fact, probably not a fifth of the measures introduced in each Congress should be treated as really "public."

Large assemblies — and Congress is no exception — are not qualified to dispense wisely either justice or mercy. History abounds in episodes showing this. By the use of committees the dangers are lessened, but when the committee reports reach the floor of the House, the judicious may well grieve. Members with no sense of proportion fritter away the precious hours in wrangling over petty payments that any competent business executive would dispose of in as many minutes. Not seldom the value to the country of the time taken, even if measured by only the proportionate share of the cost of the legislative department, far exceeds the amount involved, to say nothing of the cost that results from precluding action on really important public business. The pathetic side of it all is more distressing. Long-suffering victims of the machinery of government see their hopes of relief blasted by the watchdog of the treasury who refuses the unanimous consent usually necessary for action. Justice becomes a lottery. It is the worst aspect of the Congress of the United States.

Adding together the public and private laws and resolutions, it will be found that recent Congresses have made on an average about 750 additions to the Federal statutes — 375 a year. Taken on their face, the totals in Congress and the state legislatures furnish the theme for many a terrified editorial, essay, or speech. Some alarmists talk of the avalanche of laws; others of the deluge of legislation. Superlative epithets are exhausted. Yet anyone who will fairly analyze the output may find his apprehensions somewhat allayed.

First, he will throw out entirely or else credit with little weight the private and special laws, because they involve no basic principles of social relationship and therefore do not affect appreciably the structure or processes of society. Having thus got rid of half his problem (taking state and Federal legislation together), the investigator will next discard as unimportant a great mass of trivial changes in administrative details, not always trivial in themselves, but, as in the case of private and special laws, embodying no principle and for the most part touching the daily lives of comparatively few citizens. There is, to be sure, ground for complaint that such changes are so many and so frequent, but on the other hand there is good excuse. Just observe in factory or shop how rapidly change follows change in machinery or processes, simply because experience ever teaches improvement. No human being can foresee all the bearings of an administrative measure, can anticipate all contingencies, avoid all defects, escape all evils, be sure of having provided for the maximum of good.

Furthermore, continual change is made imperative by the march of knowledge. Applied science nowadays alters the conditions of life with a rapidity of which our fathers never dreamed, and which the reactionaries of our time seem unwilling either to comprehend or to condone. Every considerable invention creates new rights and new duties with which the legislator is likely sooner or later to have to deal.

The laws grow because the complexities of life grow. It is an age of specialization. The subdivision of labor has multiplied the conflict of interests.

The spread of schooling has vastly increased the number of self-asserting individuals, bent on pushing themselves up by pulling others down. Free scope for the competitive system under democratic conditions has vastly expanded the opportunity for the strong to exploit or oppress the weak. The inevitable corollary has been an equal growth in the scope of that prime purpose of genuine lawmaking which men have been wont to call justice. One of its aspects is that of protection; another that of fair play. It is not socialism save that it combats the anti-social evils of individualism run wild. It is paternalism only as it corresponds to the act of a father in preventing a greedy child from despoiling his brethren. It grows only because it responds to the instincts of mankind.

Observe that the complaint of too much lawmaking is generally abstract, not concrete. It comes chiefly from men who object to the mass, not to the units. Lawyers, for instance, are inconvenienced by having to keep up with changes in the statutes. Mostly, however, the fault-finders are the ultra-conservatives who by nature dislike all change. Asked to specify, they will find it embarrassing to point out in a volume of acts and resolves chapters that they can be confident were unwise. Their first impulse will be to declare this or that provision unnecessary, but when they are told the reasons, dogmatic assurance is likely to dwindle.

LAWS AND EXCEPTIONS 61

The probability is that our lawmaking bodies are really more in disfavor by reason of their omissions than of their commissions. At the end of every session much the larger part of newspaper fault-finding is based on things left undone. They are the greater cause of the scolding in the clubs, on the trains, wherever men talk about public affairs. What ought to be done is uppermost in our political campaigns, not what has been done. Many candidates solicit votes on the strength of promises to work for new laws; few pledge themselves to vote for repeals; and rare is the man who wins because he agrees to make a practice of voting "No." It would not be rash to predict that inquiry would disclose that far the greater part of the citizens who have any views whatever on such things, are dissatisfied with representative institutions because they do not accomplish more. Even those who most loudly condemn the total number of statutes, almost invariably grieve because some one measure has failed. If even the major part of these individual wishes were met, the volume of new laws would forthwith swell to alarming proportions.

The prime reason for so much denial, so much delay, is to be found in the instincts and impulses of those who control lawmaking. The truth is that the longer a man serves in legislature or Congress, the more likely he is to take the negative attitude.

He becomes familiar with the weaknesses of panaceas. He sees how often new laws bring in their train unforeseen evils more than counterbalancing their benefits. He finds that often, when no action is taken, things right themselves. In spite of himself, he becomes more and more conservative. His real need is to be on his guard against the loss of his enthusiasms.

Obstruction by the seniors is easier because to the newcomers timidity counsels inaction on proposals not of their own conception. Unfamiliarity joins in discouraging. And objectors get a more attentive hearing than proponents. Indeed, the conditions are mostly obstacles.

According to the temperament of the observer, he will find in the outcome net gain or net loss for the country as a whole. Perhaps if he be of judicial bent, he will conclude that the struggle between the forces of action and reaction results in a rate of legislative progress neither dangerously swift nor lamentably slow, but in remarkable degree corresponding to the real interest of the country.

Lecture III

SPENDING PUBLIC MONEY

BY far the greater part of the work of all the legislative bodies of the land is concerned, not with the making of genuine laws, but with the processes of that great coöperative agency we call government. This is particularly the case with Congress, as a result of the fact that by the Constitution all the powers not specifically granted to the nation were reserved to the States, and among the reserved powers are nearly all those affecting the relations of citizens with each other as individuals. Only as Congress is the governing body for the District of Columbia does it ever enact statutes touching most of the topics that fill the pages of the statute books of the states. Sometimes it frames for the District a code governing this or that activity, which it hopes may be a model for the state legislatures; but there is not enough of this to warrant calling it more than an insignificant part of the work. The genuine laws enacted under the few general powers that Congress has, would add few pages year by year to the Revised Statutes of the United States, a volume that many lawyers never have occasion to consult in the course of long practice at the bar.

The result is that probably nine tenths of the work of Congress relates to the spending of money, the regulating of the processes and practices incident thereto, and the assessing of the cost. This involves almost no questions of ethics — right and wrong. It is almost altogether matter of expediency — the common advantage, to which the interest of the individual as such must be subordinate.

The activities involved have much less of novelty in essence than is commonly supposed. When it comes to the functions of government, our day has seen no great amount of invention. Our War Department, for example, goes back to the earliest era of recorded history, and doubtless ages behind that; for association in common defence, to say nothing of offence, must have been one of the first impulses of mankind. When men began daring to ride the billows of the sea, they added a Navy Department. The Judiciary came as soon as they saw fit to regulate their private quarrels. Ambassadors and the rudiments of a Department of State followed the organization of tribes and clans. The barter stage suggested coinage, which with the need of raising money led to a Treasury Department. The benefits of united action for common conveniences were sought centuries and centuries ago in the shape of

SPENDING PUBLIC MONEY

roads, harbors, light-houses, canals, irrigation, water-works, sewers, and public buildings of many sorts, such as temples, palaces, baths, circuses. Modern times have seen the work of government broadened by adding the carriage of the mails; maintenance of hospitals; various helps to agriculture, industry, and commerce; municipal comforts in the way of lighting, transportation, parks, boulevards; and, most extensive of all, the providing of education.

There is much criticism of the spread of coöperative activity in these and other matters. The critics assume that the increase of public expenditure of all sorts, which, it must be granted, is going on with unprecedented rapidity, is in and of itself indefensible. Is the assumption valid? Who has shown that there is anything inherently wrong or even rash in the desire on the part of a people to do more work coöperatively? If the citizens conclude it is for the general welfare that private activity shall be further replaced by public activity in the support and care of the sick, the crippled, the infirm, the aged, the insane, the degenerate, does their decision in and of itself show folly? Why, if they wish, should they not invest their capital jointly in conveniences such as waterworks, bridges, highways, canals, which they have found it unwise to leave to private enterprise? Why should they not put their funds into the great works to which private capital is unequal — harbors, breakwaters, levees, irrigation dams, reclamation projects, national forests, coast and topographical surveys, sewer systems? Surely these things are matters of common concern. They have important relation to the productive capacity of the people as a whole. If after meeting their necessities men are willing to spend on their personal comforts and luxuries less than they earn, may it not be advantageous to permit them to lend, or require them to give, some part of the excess, their savings, to the instrumentality they have created to advance their joint interests, — the government, — for investment in their behalf?

Does our experience show that, as far as we have gone, this course has worked harm or been unprofitable? It is a remarkable fact that the critics are constantly generalizing about the waste of millions on millions of the public funds, yet when called on to specify, rarely can name classes of outlay they would abandon. Here and there they may point out instances of extravagance. There is much inefficiency in the conduct of public affairs, no doubt. Yet it has not been shown that on the whole the vast spread of coöperative activity in the last generation has been unwise, dangerous, or harmful. There are those of us who believe that public schools, libraries, parks, highways, boulevards, harbors,

SPENDING PUBLIC MONEY

buildings, and all other coöperations are proofs of an advancing civilization. In what does the Stone Age more contrast with ours than in respect of the capacity of men to work together? And why should not the huge increase in the wealth of the world brought by the inventions and developments of the last hundred years, be in ever-growing measure used jointly for the common welfare?

Think out the effect of the inventing and perfecting of such a thing as the telephone or the gas engine. It notably increases productivity. The gain may go to feeding more mouths — a result with benefit by no means incontestable; or to lessening the average working time — a result with more to be said in its favor, though probably most of us do not now toil a greater part of the day or year than is best for our health and real happiness. Or the gain may be used to raise the standard of living, the increase in product showing up in more of household conveniences and comforts, devices for the saving of drudgery, better clothing and more of it, the instrumentalities of recreation, and all the other material things that go to make life easier and happier. This is what the people have chiefly preferred. The advance in this direction within the last thirty years is almost incredible. Is there anything unnatural or surprising in the fact that some part of it has been made by the use of joint outlay?

68 CONGRESS—AN EXPLANATION

Of course, at any given time there must be some bound to joint expenditure. How shall it be fixed? Arbitrary limits are impracticable. Were you to search for the maximum, it would be found in the total productive capacity of the community, state, or nation. Within that maximum, and assuming beneficial purposes of common concern, the working limit may be that amount of joint expenditure which will not deprive the masses of the people of individual necessities, or of comforts or luxuries they deem more desirable than those that may be secured by joint activity. Furthermore, the wise rule restricts the scope to the things that can be better done collectively than individually, or could not otherwise be done at all.

This is necessarily vague. Precision is impossible. But in some fashion, however crude and unscientific, such a purpose is being worked out year after year by the representative assemblies of the land.

It always has been, and doubtless always will be, a piecemeal process. That would be a truism not worth voicing were it not for an aspect of legislative work seldom explained or understood. Our lawmaking bodies make beginnings infrequently. Congress engages in an absolutely new genus of outlay hardly once in a decade, an absolutely new species hardly once in each two-year term; so that occasion to pass upon what may be called the principles in-

SPENDING PUBLIC MONEY 69

volved in appropriating money is much less common than would be generally supposed. The frequent issues are those of degree rather than of basic policy.

One practical effect of this is that the great appropriation bills are not such breeders of important and prolonged debate as their bulk and the amounts involved might lead a stranger to expect. It is inevitable that accustomed kinds of outlay will be little questioned. Once a bureau is established, its life is rarely in danger. Interest lies only in the rapidity of its growth, and the advances from year to year are seldom large enough to invite keen controversy.

Improvement in the process has of late been sought by the introduction of what is known as the budget. A budget is a financial programme, to be submitted by the executive to the legislative branch. I believe in the budget in spite of most of the arguments advanced in its behalf. However well meant these arguments, however useful the end they advanced, yet if they are fallacious, they would better be abandoned, lest by getting prestige here they might do the more harm in other fields.

To proclaim the budget as a panacea for our financial ills was unnecessary and unwise. Its limitations as well as its achievements ought to be better understood.

The budget worshippers contend that presidents

and governors are much the best persons, perhaps the only competent persons, to prepare a financial programme. This might be true of a theoretical executive, constructed in the work-room of some devotee of political science, but is not necessarily nor even often true of the flesh-and-blood executives who are at the head of American states and the nation itself. Some of them have had little or no experience with the practical side of government. Others have been brought in close contact with but few of its aspects. Almost none have any wide acquaintance with the great mass of administrative detail, and the very conditions of their official being prevent them from getting such acquaintance. Other duties are too many and the days are too short. Only the most credulous imagination will conceive that a chief executive will have personal knowledge of more than a small part of the details of his budget. Very largely he must rely on the judgments of others.

It will be retorted that this is equally the case with the president of a great corporation. Advocates of the budget frequently, unnecessarily, and dangerously call on the lessons of commerce and industry to fortify their arguments. The public business does not depend for its existence on money profits at all. In American constitutional theory the government would transcend its functions if it made any money

SPENDING PUBLIC MONEY 71

profit whatever. It is a mutual benefit society, and its success is measured by service, not dividends. Furthermore, the corporation enters but one field of endeavor and its president not only is expected to be, but actually may be, an expert in that field. State and nation enter a hundred fields of endeavor, with the greatest diversity of scientific requirement. Solomon would not be wise enough to master them all. It would be folly to expect president or governor to be at the same time foremost, or even skilled, in penology and agriculture and irrigation and education and sanitation and military science and insurance and a hundred other things more or less unrelated.

Another argument is that the executive should be responsible for every detail of the financial programme because he is the man responsible for carrying out every detail. In this matter of "responsibility" great confusion prevails. Responsibility implies punishment. What could be more unjust than to require real responsibility of president or governor for the whole operation of government, to deal out to him punishment for every incapacity, every inefficiency, every failure? American common sense never has accepted, never will accept, any such idea. We do not choose our executives with it in mind; we do not pass judgment on them with it in mind. A political party may be put into office in the hope that it will better administer affairs, or be turned out because it has badly administered them, but the question is always one of totals, not of details. Only in the rarest instances do we punish any executive because of the shortcomings of minor officials. Broad policies may and should determine the fate of president or governor, but his political fortunes ought not to depend on the work of individual administrative agents.

Unless our system of government is radically unsound, a president or governor must be assumed to be the most likely to reflect the popular will on broad questions of public policy that directly affect the whole electorate, and particularly the questions uppermost in political campaigns. It follows that a proposal emanating from president or governor on a broad question of public policy, such as old-age pensions, or public ownership, or the inheritance tax, is weightier than if coming from any other source. In matters of administrative detail, however, the probabilities favor the judgments of others, and notably of the administrators who by long service or special training have become experts in their particular fields of administration, as well as the legislators who by years of work on this or that committee have become familiar with its particular problems. It may also chance that a private citizen, who has never held public office, will be better informed concerning a public need than any legislator, administrator, or executive. Taken by and large, in matters of administrative detail I should rank foremost the probabilities of wise suggestion by administrative officials; next, committee chairmen; thirdly, executives; fourthly, the mass of legislators; with the judgments of private individuals varying too much in worth to permit even an average.

Another misconception is that a budget can usefully coördinate the finances, alloting a predetermined amount of money to the various activities with proper regard to their relative importance and needs. A "scientifically equilibrated budget" is the goal. Such a budget is impossible, by reason of the very nature of government. No system can secure such a budget; no system ought to attempt to secure such a budget. Modern government tries to meet a thousand social needs. They differ as the pear and the plum, the tulip and the pansy, the song and the statue. They have no common factor, no homogeneity, often not even relationship. Only in the roughest way are comparisons possible. We may say that provision for health is more important than provision for pleasure, that the development of industry should be preferred to the development of art. But scientific adjustment is hopeless.

Equally untenable is the theory that outgo should

be made dependent on income. Here again the analogy of corporation processes does not hold. At the beginning of the fiscal year the business corporation commands, or can foresee with some accuracy that it will or may command, a certain amount of capital which can be used for such purposes as commend themselves. The limitation is fairly definite. The capital and surplus to start the year with are known; the borrowing capacity is determined by the assets; the only uncertain factor is the net income from the business, and an approximate estimate of this is usually feasible. So the directors can easily say: "We will spend such-and-such an amount next year." They can lay out a budget accordingly. They both can and must cut the coat according to the cloth.

The same thing is largely true of municipal corporations where statutes restrict the tax-rate and the borrowing power. It is less the case with cities that have a free hand, though even they are a good deal restrained, by the force of a local opinion that quickly reaches the council. Upon state legislatures public opinion acts much less effectively, and no compulsion has made it customary for them to set a limit in advance save where now and then a governor has announced that he would veto measures putting the aggregate above a given figure. With the national government the influence of public opinion on appropriations virtually disappears. Some control by the executive is possible through the exercise of sundry powers that attach to the office, and their use has of late been shown to be capable of material effect in securing specific economies, with of course a corresponding effect on totals; but this has not been due to such tangible restraints as control business corporations.

There is another essential difference between the circumstances of a business enterprise and those of a political body. Most corporations can, if they choose, double or halve their outlay in a single year. Our cities and states never do that sort of thing, nor does the nation unless forced to it by the exigencies of war. Public expenditure grows by short steps, or occasionally may be reduced in small degree. So predetermination of the year's outlay, with its allotment following, is much more natural for a board of directors than for a city council, state legislature, or Congress. In other words, there does not exist the same occasion for it in the two classes of activities.

In preliminary balancing of income and outgo Congress would find especial difficulty due to the fact that the national revenue must largely come from indirect taxation. Cities can easily change the tax-rate on real estate from year to year. States can likewise without incidental harm alter corporation or inheritance taxes frequently. But the business world would see disaster in annual change of the tariff. It would also be a misfortune for Congress itself if a revision of the whole money-raising scheme or any considerable part of it were a yearly necessity.

As a result of all these reasons, our lawmakers of all grades have come to think it natural, logical, and reasonable to determine outgo first, income afterward. It is not the fact that this necessarily, or indeed usually, results in extravagance. The system is not inconsistent with prudence, economy, or restraint. What actually takes place in American legislative processes is that, when the total of appropriation bids fair to result in a tax increase larger than the people are likely to stand without partisan revolt, whoever has the authority starts in to prune — sometimes the president or governor by the use of the veto, sometimes the legislative committee by cutting down or cutting out items of the general appropriation bill, or the legislative leaders by killing sundry appropriations.

This is, of course, quite unscientific. It is the crude, inexact method of all legislative procedure. It is the survival of the strongest, not necessarily of the fittest. The budget facilitates the elimination of the proposals having the fewest friends. It helps the measuring of favor, and as the scale of favor determined by the struggles and compromises of the forum is our accepted way of converting popular judgment into action, whatever helps the measuring of favor is worth while. Yet it is a vain hope that the budget will do more than lessen somewhat the irregularities of public economy.

More illogical is the widespread demand that expenditure shall be coördinated with revenue. The readiness with which this demand has been accepted is most remarkable. It has become almost a commonplace in the language of the reformers. They rank it high in the scale of the changes that must be made if the country is to be saved. Yet it is a demand that takes no account of the facts in the conduct of American government. Our way — it may not be the best way, but it is our way — is to look first at details, letting aggregates take care of themselves. We decide in each particular what we think we ought to have, and we add our separate decisions to find what shall be the total of taxation. Here again the lessons of the commercial world or of individual experience are mischievously misleading. A business firm or corporation expects to invest all its capital. Most individuals spend all or nearly all their earnings. On the contrary a state or a nation impresses but a small part of the capital within its borders, spends but a small part of the income of its citizens. In practical effect its resources, compared with the needs now viewed as normal by men not Socialists or Communists, are limitless. No total of ordinary expenditure likely to meet with acceptance would approach the limit of resources. Therefore the really determining question for state or nation is never, "Can we afford it?" but, "How badly do we want it?"

Another of the delusive arguments for the budget rests on the vain hope that a systematic presentation of the financial programme will secure the help of public scrutiny and criticism. The consummation is devoutly to be wished, but why take time for dreaming of it? The newspapers, edited by keen men whose very livelihood depends on publishing what the sovereign citizen wants to read, no longer describe or discuss in detail the serious doings of our legislators. The newspaper judgment is that the sovereign citizen takes no interest in these doings and will not read about them. Ordinarily no information reaches a constituency regarding the action of its representative on any proposed expenditure. At rare intervals a community believing itself overburdened by taxation will rise in its majesty and blindly smite anybody it can reach. Then it relapses into indifference. No tabulation of dreary figures will have any charm for Mr. Average Citizen. Better put "Publicity" up on the shelf with "Responsibility."

Not even is it true that in the hands of the mass of legislators themselves the Budget, or Book of Estimates, or whatever it may be called, has any practical value. Theorists argued with confidence, with conviction, that if at the opening of the session each member had before him a comprehensive statement in detail of the whole financial programme, he would study it and so prepare himself for the debates and votes on the various appropriation bills. There is no element of confession in the statement that I have found not the slightest use in the huge volume delivered to me annually for this purpose. Nor have I ever heard any other member say he found it of use. It may help members of the Committee on Appropriations, though my suspicion is that they examine only the pages relating to the work of the sub-committees on which they serve. Perhaps it is examined by the very few men who have a flair for checking up the work of the Committee on Appropriations and conceive it a duty to pick flaws in its reports — very rarely, by the way, with practical results. The great bulk of the other Senators and Representatives hoist the thing to a top shelf on the chance that they may want to refer to it some time, which in my case has never happened. This is not because of indifference or neglect. We simply have not the time to meet the expectations of the budgetary enthusiasts. Only by chance do we know the facts behind the figures. We feel ourselves lost in the deluge of dollars. It is hopeless.

Fortunately it is not necessary to rely on false analogies or mistaken conceptions to prove the desirability of the essential parts of the budget reform. It is quite defensible as an orderly fiscal programme, securing preliminary study, proper accounting, and specific economies in matters of detail. In Congress the sub-committees of the Committee on Appropriations make as thorough and careful study as the conditions permit, and it is admirable, but it must be done in a comparatively short time and therefore with more haste than is desirable. The Bureau of the Budget is at work the year round. Its task of looking for chances to economize in spending money already appropriated, by preventing duplication and other waste, brings knowledge of how to lessen future appropriation. Furthermore there is distinct gain from independent study by the Budget Commissioner. Bringing before him the officials responsible for the estimates, and speaking in the name of their chief, the President, he can exert more influence than Congress in the all-important particular, which is at the heart of the whole problem, namely, the judgment of the man carrying on the work that may be in question. Nobody else can know so well as he what should be spent to do this work both effectively and economically. The first task both of the

SPENDING PUBLIC MONEY

Budget Commissioner and of Congress is to get this man to tell the truth. The temptation is strong for him to ask more than he needs, through fear of having his request cut anyhow. He may be honestly ignorant of what is the truth, through failure to have studied the possibilities of employing fewer clerks or stopping useless labor or getting along with less in the way of supplies. If he knows he is to be put on the rack by a budget commissioner, he will take thought against this, or failing so to do, he may at the inquiry disclose his inability to justify his figures and will find them sharply reduced.

In Washington the battle over economy is not between the President and Congress, but between the President and his administrators. Each head of a department or bureau has an honorable and laudable ambition to advance the interest that is his chief concern for the time, or indeed may be his life-work. Inevitably he magnifies the importance of his own task. Inevitably he seeks for more power, and that means more helpers and more money.

Congress, on the other hand, is distinctly penurious. Somehow men are less generous in the mass than as individuals. Many a plebiscite involving salaries has proved this. In any legislative assembly you will find plenty of business men who are more careful of the public money than they would be of their own. Congress does cheese-paring after the

Budget Commissioner has finished. In each of the last three years the appropriations have been more than $10,000,000 below the budget figures. Contrast this with the statement made by the English Committee on National Expenditure in 1918, that there had not been a single instance in the preceding twenty-five years when the House of Commons by its own direct action had reduced on financial grounds any estimate submitted.

Yet Congress has a reputation for waste and extravagance that is notorious. Why this injustice, so wide of the facts? It is partly because in all times and in all countries where representative government has prevailed, many of the people have taken a keen delight in abusing their representatives. It is partly an inheritance from days when the standards of public service were far below what they are to-day. For example, undoubtedly there was once a "pork-barrel," a metaphorical barrel from which legislators pulled out "pork" to satisfy the ravenous appetites of greedy constituents. There is no longer any pork-barrel and there has been none for years. Yet the memory survives in what is now little else than sheer slander.

The baneful fiction is attached chiefly to two classes of expenditure — one for the improvement of rivers and harbors, the other for the erection of public buildings. The charge is that untold millions

SPENDING PUBLIC MONEY

are wasted despite the protest of the few honest men in House and Senate, against the advice of the government experts, and to the abhorrence of the whole administration.

What are the facts?

When a Congressman thinks that money should be spent on a river or harbor in his district, he must first persuade a committee to recommend and the House to agree that a survey shall be made. This must be repeated in the other branch. If that were the whole story, there might be just criticism, for so far attention to the project will have been largely perfunctory. The story, however, has only begun. Now comes the technician, assumed, and usually with right, to be expert, unprejudiced, disinterested, honorable. The Chief of Engineers of the War Department, through his staff, which is supposed to be composed of very capable engineers, directs a preliminary examination to be made by a district officer. If this officer is convinced by his examination that the project would be useful and probably ought to be undertaken, then a regular survey is authorized, followed by an estimate of cost. If the report is again favorable, it goes to the Board of Engineers for Rivers and Harbors, consisting of seven men, a brigadier general, colonels, and majors, all of practical experience in this field. They make careful examination. If they in turn favor, their report must be approved by the Chief of Engineers before recommendation will be sent to Congress by the Secretary of War.

The Budget Committee of 1919 was made up of some of the ablest men in the House, men of long experience and the highest standing. They were agreed that not in their time had a single expenditure for improvement of river or harbor been advised by the Committee on Appropriations unless it had been recommended by the army engineers and approved by the Secretary of War.

No unprejudiced man can deny that in the last ten years the total of appropriations for rivers and harbors has been far below what the needs of commerce and the prosperity of the nation would have justified.

In the matter of public buildings Congress has been still more shortsighted and miserly. It is grossly wasteful in the extent to which it persists in paying rentals rather than build. Much work is carried on under crowded conditions that are bad economy. Not since 1913 has there been a public building bill. One was attempted in the 68th Congress (1923–1925), for the purpose of meeting the unbusinesslike, deplorable situation, but it failed of passage. The episode added to the reasons why, if Congress is to be blamed, it should be for parsimony and not for extravagance.

SPENDING PUBLIC MONEY

Another misconception about Congress is that, in the face of the recommendations of its committees and against their protests, it greatly increases the appropriations by amendments on the floor. Logrolling is alleged to be a habit. Importunity and favor are supposed to waste millions. The fact, however, is that the House rules make it very difficult, indeed usually impossible, to add or enlarge by amendment. Senate rules are not so strict, and the Senate appears to be by nature more liberal than the House. In fact, most Representatives would be likely to put it more uncharitably and say that the Senate is the less careful, cautious, and economical body. Anyhow, the man who thinks that the House has been stingy, tries to get a Senator to move to amend by inserting what the House has omitted, or increasing what it has voted. The result is that a good many increases or new items go from the Senate to the inevitable conference committee. In practice this institution long resulted in giving the Senate its way much more often than the House relished; but of late that has been checked by a new House rule forbidding its conferees, unless specifically authorized by separate vote, to agree to any Senate amendment that would have violated the House rule had it been offered in the House. As the House rule thus controlling is very strict, the Senate is no longer able to force appropriations that do not commend themselves to the House.

Records for many years show that the net increase of appropriations on the floor, beyond the committee reports, has been less than one tenth of one per cent. Most of this was undoubtedly for purposes about which honest and sincere men might well differ in judgment. The figures explain why, at least in Congress, no great importance attaches to one of the most mooted issues in the matter of budget reform, that of executive control. In Parliament no member may move to increase a single item of expenditure as proposed by the government, that is to say, the ministry. Not a few friends of the budget reform have insisted that the same rule should be put in force here. Congress in enacting the system refused to abdicate its powers in this particular. It has seen no occasion to regret the decision. Its self-respect was worth saving. It is chosen to carry out the will of the people and ought not to shirk its responsibility. That in matter of thrift it on the whole meets this responsibility in praiseworthy degree, should be the verdict of every fair-minded observer.

How far it may be the duty of Congress to concern itself with the expenditure of the money appropriated, is a difficult problem, to which curiously little attention has been paid. The Constitution is quite silent on the subject, save only in the provisions about impeachment so far as they bring in the matter under "high crimes and misdemeanors."

SPENDING PUBLIC MONEY

The legislative branch of course may and should watch the other branches with a view to future appropriations as well as to the need of legislation; but has it any responsibility whatever in the matter of how what has already been appropriated is spent? Apparently it has been taken for granted that such responsibility exists. The public seems to have a vague notion to that effect, and it is not lacking in Congress itself, for matters of maladministration are broached there from time to time, and the lower branch has committees on expenditures in the various departments. These committees, however, rarely make any attempt to function, and nobody seems to have a clear idea why they exist or what they should do.

Five sixths of the state constitutions specify in varying language that the three departments of government — legislative, executive, and judicial — shall be distinct. The other constitutions would doubtless be construed to imply the same thing, as always has been done in the case of the Federal Constitution. What business, then, has the legislative branch with the way the executive branch functions, except as legislation and appropriation are concerned?

Of course, the situation is quite different in those countries where ministerial responsibility is the keystone of government. There the committee of the legislative branch that constitutes the Cabinet, is made up mostly if not entirely of heads of executive departments. They may properly be questioned in the legislative body as to what they are doing in the way of executing the laws. Nothing of the sort is theoretically justifiable under our system of division of powers; it would not be feasible without reconstruction of our legislative systems; and there is grave doubt whether it would be desirable. Congress already fails to convince the nation that it does efficiently its recognized part of the work of government. Were there to be added the task of inquiry into the processes of administration, for the purpose of securing greater economy and efficiency in the execution of existing law and the spending of money already appropriated, then of necessity it could give less time and thought to its well-established functions.

It will be argued that congressional investigations of what are commonly called scandals in the executive departments have served to correct flagrant abuses, to punish notorious culprits, and to raise the standards of public service. The accuracy of this must not be taken for granted. Congressional committees rarely adopt even the most familiar precautions of courts of justice, the practice taught by centuries of experience as necessary for the protection of persons accused and for ascertainment of the

SPENDING PUBLIC MONEY

truth. The partisan factor is liable to vitiate the procedure and make the findings deceptive if not wholly worthless. Justice never is to be sought in legislative chambers — sometimes equity, but never exact justice. That is to be found only in the courts.

To the individual member the problem of his relation to the executive departments brings difficulties and embarrassments. Many of his constituents believe it his duty to secure the adoption of their views in the conduct of the public business. They may, for instance, ask him to concern himself with even so small a matter as the location of a mail box on a free delivery route, expecting to get him to use his influence for over-ruling the decision of the subordinate who may have passed judgment. Members of Congress are always glad to help a constituent place his opinions or wishes before the right official; but when it comes to the use of influence for upsetting the normal administrative procedure, interfering with discipline, getting special favors, or otherwise infringing on the responsibilities of the executive branch, the Congressman who has respect for the principles of good government hesitates.

Through many years much trouble and harm came from the relation of members to appointments to office. These were viewed as political perquisites. The adoption of the merit system, commonly referred to as civil service reform, has vastly bettered the situation. Nowadays there is almost no office, except that of postmaster, which a Massachusetts Representative has any share in filling. Arrangements differ in other states, but, speaking broadly, it may be said that, again barring postmasters, the members of the House are not greatly burdened by office-seekers. To Senators of the party in power trouble is still brought by the higher positions in the public service, but their load is nothing like what it was half a century ago. Too many persons, however, still remain unconvinced. They are not informed as to how far the merit system has been extended, or if knowing the rules, refuse to believe that these are genuinely and sincerely enforced. So they ask the Congressman to use what they assume to be his influence. It would be extravagant to say that minor appointments are never now thus affected, but it is within bounds to aver that in few other fields of regulatory and prohibitory enactment is there to-day less evasion.

What little trouble survives in respect to the great mass of positions that have been brought under the Civil Service rules, develops chiefly in the matter of promotions, especially in the postal and customs services. Many subordinates still believe, and sometimes with good ground, that their chances for preferment hinge on political influence. Perhaps another half century must pass before all occasion for

SPENDING PUBLIC MONEY

this belief disappears. Meanwhile the Congressman must expect embarrassment if he feels that he ought to let the executive branch alone.

Singularly enough, however, not a few Congressmen apparently have no wish to keep their hands off the administration of the laws. They are at heart hostile to Civil Service reform and are believers in the spoils system. It is possible that there is no legislative body in the land which, if it could act by secret, unrecorded ballot, would not throw Civil Service reform out of the window. Some legislators sincerely believe that no stereotyped examination can match personal judgment in the selection of either public or private servants. Others begrudge what they think the loss of political power and individual advantage, though as a matter of fact it may be at least questioned whether a share in appointments is not more of a liability than an asset. Gratitude is far weaker than ingratitude. The favor that makes one friend and a dozen enemies does not help much in the long run. Then, too, why any man in public life should urge return to the days when office-seekers took a quarter or more of a Congressman's time and kept him constantly in hot water, is hard to comprehend. However, the reform has come to stay. In my own judgment the sooner it is complete, the better.

With its help and with the rise in the standards of

public service, it is possible that no country in the world now surpasses ours in governmental efficiency. Certainly observation and report indicate that we are in this matter ahead of most other nations. We may differ as to the wisdom of this or that class of expenditure, but that the money once appropriated is on the whole honestly and efficiently expended, cannot be fairly gainsaid. This of course means such efficiency as the conditions of governmental employment permit. Everybody knows that from public service cannot by and large be expected as much as from private service. The lack of incentive, the absence of great rewards, the security of tenure, these and other considerations ensure that the political system cannot equal the competitive system in the material results of individual accomplishment. Which system may for other reasons work the larger sum total of benefit, is of course another question.

Raising money to pay the cost of government is the necessary complement to spending money. Outgo compels income. So the second great task of Congress is to levy taxes or borrow funds. The levying of taxes has been a prolific source of political dispute, frequently furnishing the main issue in national campaigns, whereas the spending of money has rarely invited partisan controversy. One result is that the work of the Committee on Appropriations is non-partisan, while that of the Committee on

SPENDING PUBLIC MONEY

Ways and Means is just the opposite. The big tariff bills are usually agreed upon by the majority members of the Committee on Ways and Means, and then submitted perfunctorily to the minority members, who can do nothing but protest there and criticise on the floor of the House. It must not be supposed that these bills are the hasty work of amateurs. On the contrary, they are the product of the best expert advice that can be commanded to carry out the general purpose of the political party happening to be in power.

Taxation measures have not in our time been so essentially political as tariff bills. The conditions of the World War precluded partisanship in the drafting of the laws necessary to raise the vast sums required. Naturally since then neither party has been able to find in the principles each had accepted a major political issue. On the controverted features of the income tax, the votes in the House do not yet follow party lines closely enough to let praise or blame be focussed.

Measures relating to the borrowing of funds have been still less partisan. They have in them, however, the seeds of important political strife, and the question of the speed with which our huge war debt shall be paid off may presently stir classes and masses of the people into sharp controversy.

Lecture IV

LEADERSHIP

MANKIND always wants and must have leadership in government. Men cannot well function politically in the mass. They must entrust power to one or a few of their number. For centuries the resort, whether by active consent or passive acceptance, was for the most part to one man — a monarch. Occasionally and in a few places we know of division of authority, as in the Greek city states for a time, and in Rome under the consulate. Absolute monarchy, however, was the general thing until after the Normans had conquered England. Under the Norman kings Parliament was born. Since then Englishmen have developed two new types of leadership, which in our day have come to prevail in much the greater part of the civilized world. Their nature merits study, in part because of their intrinsic interest, in part because our country is almost alone in maintaining one of these types, and is now being strongly urged to abandon it in favor of the other.

It was in the seventeenth century that England made much of its progress from government by one man to government by a few men. Under the Tudors Parliament had well-nigh disappeared. James the First stoutly resisted all attacks on his absolute powers. In the struggle by others for a share in control, Charles the First lost his head. With the return of the Stuarts after the Cromwellian episode, absolutism again took the saddle, only to be thrown off by the Revolution that brought William of Orange to England. It was William who found it prudent to choose all his advisers from one political party. Under his successor, Queen Anne, the ministers came to be recognized as responsible to Parliament. Under George the First, largely through the accident that he could not speak English, the power of the cabinet grew apace. An admitted leader, a prime minister, came into being, in the person of Sir Robert Walpole, not by deliberate intention on anybody's part, but because he so towered above the rest that power inevitably centred in him. Reaction followed in the early years of the reign of George the Third, but his resistance was vain. When our Federal Constitution was framed, it had come to be accepted in England that a cabinet should ordinarily be composed of members of the same political party; should be of a party controlling a majority in the House of Commons; should resign when no longer supported by a majority; should look to the people for ultimate authority; should be responsible for all the acts of government; and should have a commanding head, the prime minister.

The next hundred years saw the wane of Parliament as an initiating body. By the middle of the nineteenth century, individual members of the House had ceased going beyond calling proposals to the attention of the government. A generation later it had become the practice for the ministry to determine upon all the important legislation before Parliament even assembled. With the passage of still another generation, the process of giving to the cabinet the monopoly of initiation was completed. Now no member of a minority, no independent member, if there be such, can hope for consideration of any proposal he may present. Indeed, the ministers have so monopolized the time that no member of the majority not in the government has more than a gambler's chance of getting so much as an insignificant measure considered. Not even by way of amendment may the private member embody his own ideas in legislation unless the government approves or permits. Discussion has dwindled in importance. To-day it may be said of the English Cabinet that, besides being the chief executive and central administrative board of the nation, it is in effect the lawmaking body; that of its own initiative and upon its own responsibility it makes the laws, modified only as the criticisms of Parliament may be accepted, and subject to veto only if it loses its majority in the House of Commons; that it shapes the programme and directs the procedure of Parliament; that, save for the opportunity to criticize or vote in opposition, the member of Parliament not in the cabinet is a negligible factor; and that inasmuch as the prime minister necessarily dominates the cabinet he is virtually an autocrat, controlled by an unwritten Constitution which obliges him to act within the law, and having duration of power contingent upon the popular will.

This is the form of government commended to the American people by many academic writers as preferable to that under which we now live. We are urged to approach it by modifying our congressional and executive practices so that we shall have one-man leadership and control. We are told by not a few publicists that this way alone does our salvation lie. From time to time steps in this direction have actually been taken.

To weigh the merit of the advice and the wisdom of the tendency, first consider how and why our radically different system came into existence.

Through a century and a half the American colonies quarrelled with their governors appointed by the Crown. More than any other one cause, these quarrels brought the Revolution. Our fathers went into the Revolutionary War embittered against executive authority. They fought it and they won it without any chief executive. As a result of their own experience, they framed their state constitutions with the deliberate intention of keeping the executive down to at least a level with the legislative. With serious, careful premeditation they devised a balance of powers. The very foundation of their frames of government was the doctrine that no one branch of the government should dominate. Measured by the results in the totality of everything that concerns the safety of the state and the welfare of its citizens, who will aver that the system worked out from the experience of the first century and a half of the American people has not, on the whole, been justified in the experience of the succeeding century and a half?

Again and again in the course of this period numbers of the citizens have struggled to throw off the shackles put on them by their constitutions, to rid themselves of their responsibilities, to abdicate their power in favor of a single one of their number. At times it would seem as if nearly all of even the more thoughtful part of the community despaired of democracy and longed to renounce its principle. What is the prime demand of real democracy? Is it not that every citizen shall share in the duties as well as the privileges of government? And is it not the citizen's first duty to contribute his judgment to the common stock? Yet independent judgment is the last thing that many critics now wish even in the men chosen ostensibly to represent their fellows in this very particular. Leadership, by which is commonly meant dictatorship, is the demand. Dictatorship may be the best form of government, but it is not democracy. Maybe Senators and Representatives who incline to do their own thinking are derelict and blameworthy; but that was what the men who wrote the Constitution intended they should do. Perhaps the work of those men was a failure, but under it this country has risen to great heights of prosperity and power.

Watching the recurrent attacks upon independent judgment, each seemingly more vigorous than the one before, the philosophical observer may well wonder whether the mass of mankind is really at heart in sympathy with democracy, and whether democracy will long satisfy the instincts of any state. With half our possible electors failing to go to the polls, with four fifths of the other half always voting as directed by a party label, with many of the remaining fifth demanding that the chosen representatives shall blindly follow somebody or other, where is the proof that we really want our laws to embody and our government to apply the self-exercised judgment of many minds?

Perhaps, though, the attractions of dictatorship will not in the end prevail. We chance to be in a period when their praise is conspicuous. It will doubtless be followed, as it has been preceded, by periods with independence uppermost. Such was the quarter-century following the revolt of the colonies. When the popular craving for a master reasserted itself, curiously enough the first President to take advantage of it was one who had been a leader among the opponents of executive authority, Thomas Jefferson. Next of the willing autocrats was another who gave lip-service to the rights and duties of the individual man — Andrew Jackson, who mastered Congress and ruled the country with a rod of iron for eight years. Whether Abraham Lincoln would have controlled had it not been for the dictatorial authority necessarily imposed on him by the conditions of war, no man can say with confidence; but in view of his conciliatory temperament and in the light of the part Congress actually played in governmental affairs all through the Civil War, it seems probable that under peace conditions Lincoln would have been no autocrat. Cleveland was of a more domineering type, and men close to McKinley say that, despite his suavity, no President before his time had so successfully managed Congress. Roosevelt was a born leader, and Wilson easily moulded a subservient Congress

LEADERSHIP

to his will. Three quarters of our Presidents, however, have thought it their duty to execute rather than make the laws. Of course that way of putting it must be understood to take into account the constitutional injunction that the President shall recommend to the consideration of Congress such measures as he shall judge necessary and expedient. That which goes beyond recommendation is the debatable share in the making of laws.

The issue was brought into the forum of serious discussion by a little book called "Congressional Government," published just forty years ago and written by Woodrow Wilson, then a graduate student at Johns Hopkins University. In this vigorous volume he urged the superiority of a responsible cabinet ministry over committee government, as he called that by the Congress of the United States. The book has been read by probably most of the students of political science who have since then gone through our colleges, and its doctrine has been championed by effective writers, conspicuous among them Professor H. J. Ford of Princeton, who has taken every opportunity to press the argument that the system devised by our forefathers was unwise and that we should supplant it with the English system. Meanwhile few have wielded the cudgels in defence of the American system.

The result is that now in the scholastic world it

seems to be taken for granted that the doctrine of the separation of powers is moribund if not already dead. In the legislative world, however, where practical men do the day's work, observation and experience still keep that doctrine very much alive. We who have to deal daily with the administration of government are by no means confident that our fathers were all wrong in what they did. Most of us, on the contrary, become more and more convinced that, at any rate under American conditions, it is well that the laws should not be made and executed by the same man or the same small group of men. Assuming then for the moment that the question is still open, consider the arguments.

Cabinet government is chiefly extolled because it is said to centre responsibility. By this it is meant that one man may well be held responsible for the policies and the practices of the national government, both legislative and administrative, with reward or penalty for himself or his party as may be adjudged by the voters at the following election. The theory is that the processes of election result directly in the choice of an American President, or indirectly in the choice of a British Prime Minister, who will better express and more effectively carry out the will of the majority than would Congress or Parliament left to its own devices. In support of the theory it is argued that a chief executive should be at the same time a chief legislative, because he has the more comprehensive and better proportioned conception of the interests of all the people; that he is more quickly responsive to changes in public opinion; and that he will reach decision more promptly, prudently, and bravely.

While it may be that the head of the nation, coming in contact with well-informed and judicious men from all parts of the land, will get a better perspective than any one Senator or Representative, the theory of representative government is that his knowledge will not be so comprehensive as the united knowledge of five or six hundred men chosen by states or districts, each familiar with local needs, wishes, opinions. Furthermore, it would be unreasonable to expect that in the matter of proportion a president could excel the joint acquaintance of a Congress. Inevitably he meets chiefly men from the upper walks of life. They are what we call the successful men, the dominant men. Very likely it is best that their counsel should be the loudest, but in point of proportion it would hardly be thought as representative as that of a Congress in which every stratum of society has its voice, as well as every important occupation, with every member passing some months of each year among his constituents.

As to speed in response to change of public opinion, there are arguments both ways. Unquestionably any legislative body left to itself is more conservative, more cautious, than a small group such as a cabinet would be. Congress is sluggish. Yet there are some advantages in making haste slowly. It was the tortoise who won in the race with the hare. Congress lags behind the thinkers of the nation. But the thinkers are few in comparison with the great mass of mankind, which is by nature conservative and reactionary. Much is to be said for the proposition that Congress on the whole moves as fast as the nation really wishes. Studied in detail, however, the work will be found in sundry particulars clearly and unfortunately behindhand. Were the responsibility centred in one virile, forceful man, this would doubtless be remedied.

Such a man would reach decision more promptly than Congress, and perhaps more bravely, but whether more prudently, is not so sure. It would depend on the man. Everybody is thankful that Jefferson put through the Louisiana Purchase and Roosevelt the Panama Canal, but most men will agree that the prudence of Jackson's treatment of the United States Bank, with its contribution to the panic of 1837, is gravely to be doubted. A wise despot is the best of rulers, a foolish despot the worst. The men who wrote our Constitution knew well George the Third. To be sure, the cabinet system produces prime ministers far above most

LEADERSHIP

hereditary monarchs in point of intellectual capacity, and so does our system of choosing presidents, but neither guarantees against the possibility of rashness in some critical juncture. It was to guard against imprudence that our fathers devised constitutions, state and federal, of checks and balances. They knew human nature, its frailties as well as its virtues. Is it certain that they erred in judgment when they sought safety in numbers?

Over against the arguments for the cabinet system are to be set certain other formidable considerations, to my mind not often squarely met by its advocates. First may be put the belief of the framers of our constitutions that the fusion of functions invites tyranny. To be sure it is an old-time belief, but a belief is not necessarily fallacious because it is old. Experience may in the past have taught mankind at least a few things that are still useful. It has been the experience of many states that when the man who makes the law also administers and adjudicates it, oppression is likely to result. Abuse of power has been a characteristic of monarchs.

In the last analysis cabinet government, at the stage it has reached in England to-day, is nothing but monarchy under another name, and pretty near absolute monarchy at that while it lasts; for the Parliament can at a moment's notice change any and every precept in the unwritten Constitution of

Great Britain, and the Parliament acts at the will of the Prime Minister as long as he is in power. Fortunately the courts of England function with courage. They do not, indeed, deny theoretical omnipotence in Parliament, but who will doubt that if need arose, they would find a way to thwart some palpable attempt to work gross injustice by statute? Furthermore, Parliament itself is dominated by a most powerful body of tradition and precedent, built up through many centuries, making swift action by radical forces well-nigh impossible. When a Labor ministry came into office, its Prime Minister evidently dared not attempt more than an extremely moderate programme of action.

England itself is a compact state of small area, inhabited by a homogeneous people. Is it certain that the success of one-man government under such conditions could be duplicated in a huge country like ours, with a widely scattered population made up of the most diverse racial elements, and without any universally recognized body of tradition and precedent? England's prime ministers found it impossible to handle the Roman Catholic population of Ireland. They make no attempt to control the affairs of Canada or Australasia. They are lessening their share in those of India. Does this not at least suggest that, where national interests are diverse, conflicting, and scattered, safety and success lie in a form of government whereunder the decisions are to be made by the compromises of a legislative assembly rather than by the judgment of one man or any small group of men?

Apart from such questions of basic principle, there is at least one practical consideration that seems to me of great consequence. Our system does give the opportunity for many minds to help. Every member of Congress has the chance to contribute toward good legislation. If he belong to the majority party, he is not necessarily a voting dummy as in Parliament; if he belong to the minority, he is not restricted to mere fault-finding, as Mr. Wilson wanted him to be, but in the committee room may play a most useful part in constructive effort for the public good. It should always be remembered that, anyhow, only a few big questions, if any, call for aggressive political leadership. The great mass of the business of every lawmaking body is non-partisan in nature. To sacrifice all the benefit of our parliamentary system in respect of much the larger part of the work for the sake of getting some other way of determining a very few major issues, might be a costly bargain.

Also it should be remembered that no chief executive has the time or strength to study thoroughly and to master by himself more than a few of the important problems of government. He must perforce rely largely on the judgment and advice of others. Naturally and properly in matters affecting the work of any of the departments he will turn to his cabinet officers. For a concrete illustration, take the aircraft-battleship controversy. On this the man presumably best qualified to inform and advise the President is the Secretary of the Navy. In theory that is the reason for the presence of the Secretary of the Navy in the Cabinet. Were the principle of responsible leadership to prevail completely in a matter like this, the opinion of the Secretary of the Navy, when approved by the President, would be enacted into law, the majority in Congress acquiescing without demur. The practical question, then, is whether the opinion of the Secretary of the Navy is likely to be sounder, wiser, better than that of the two committees of Congress concerned with naval affairs, one composed of sixteen Senators and the other composed of twenty-one members of the House. It chances that the House Chairman has been a member of Congress for twenty-eight years, and through much if not all of that time has been in touch with naval problems. Other members have had long acquaintance with what has become their specialty. Who will better appraise the views of the subordinates in the navy, with whom the information and the opinion must originate? Do the facts leave it clear that committee government in such a case is necessarily inferior to cabinet government?

LEADERSHIP

But it is argued that as the President is at the centre of the administration, he is in a better position than any other one man to be informed about all of its functions and operations. Of course, that is true, but it would be the height of cruelty to demand that he take full advantage of his opportunity. He simply could not do it. The task would kill him. The 531 members of Senate and House, divided into groups of specialists, are not fully equal to such achievement. Why expect it of one man?

The rejoinder of the moderate and judicious advocate of responsible leadership will fairly be that its principle may not justly be thus reduced to absurdity, inasmuch as only dominant leadership in broad matters of policy is really asked. Confined within such limits, the question is more debatable. Yet even here it would be hard to show that in actual results the British system works better than ours. As a matter of fact, the influence of the President is great, as it ought to be. No man reaches that high office unless he has outstanding qualities which make for leadership. The President is sure to be a man of patriotic purpose, deeply conscious of his solemn obligation to make decision with a sole view to the welfare of all the people. He is also sure to have had wide and long experience in dealing with his fellows. The circumstances of his relations with the legislative branch are such that his policies are ensured sympathetic and generous consideration. Ordinarily he prevails, though the public does not think so, because its attention is limited to the comparatively few instances in which he does not prevail. We do have effective and responsible presidential leadership to a very material degree. But Congress is not disposed to abandon entirely its share of initiative, or to abdicate, even in the broadest matters of policy, its function as the legislative branch of the government. Nor can the intelligent observer be confident that it could wisely be compelled so to do by constitutional change reorganizing our form of government on the British model.

Change of the Constitution would not be necessary for adoption of one feature of the cabinet system that has been admired and envied by not a few able Americans, statesmen as well as theorists. A simple change in the rules would permit members of the President's Cabinet to attend the sittings of Congress in order to make speeches and to answer questions, though not to vote. It is argued that this would tend to more of harmony between the legislative and executive branches, and would furnish a better way than now exists for putting the information and opinion of the heads of departments at the command of Congress.

Whether more of harmony between the branches is desirable may not be so clear as it would seem at

LEADERSHIP

first glance. Something is to be said for the benefits of hostility in moderate degree. Friction has its advantages in statecraft as well as in mechanics. The rivalries encouraged by the present system, the antagonisms, yes, even the controversies, invigorate and stimulate. If, however, more could be said for peace and good-will, yet the presence of Cabinet officers on the floors of Congress might militate against such an end more than it would help. To dream of sympathetic, generous treatment of the unlucky department head when the opportunity to worry and embarrass and browbeat would be so alluring, is idle. Inside the chambers the advantage would be with the questioners. Outside, an equally undesirable advantage would accrue the other way, for the public, always sympathizing with the under-dog, always admiring the one man who contends against many, would lend a ready ear to the arguments of the Cabinet member, and pay no attention to the opposing considerations. The speech of the Secretary would be sent out in advance and widely printed. Speeches in reply would if made in the House never get into print, save in the Congressional Record, and if in the Senate would be so condensed by the editors as to have little effect. So the executive branch would get another powerful instrument for swaying public opinion.

On the floor the Cabinet member would present a

pitiful spectacle if he had no capacity for public speaking. The result would be to confine the President's choice of Cabinet members to men gifted with the power of eloquence, or at least with some experience in the art. Such qualification is not now necessary, and many secretaries without it have given notable public service. Indeed, the qualities of an orator usually denote unfitness for such work as that, say, of a Secretary of the Treasury. That is why there would be distinct loss to our public life if the silent men should be precluded from serving as the heads of the great business departments of the government.

If constant or frequent attendance were required, it would be a sad invasion of time now none too plentiful for the performance of official duties. Were the ordinary attendance of a Cabinet officer restricted by custom to the days when the appropriation bill affecting his department was up, of course no serious harm in this respect would follow, but this would not meet the ideas of those who want spokesmen for the administration always on hand to defend its policies both in general and in particular. Also it would not permit the practice of questions, much extolled by some writers on political science. Other critics, however, doubt the value of questioning, and anyhow it is a time-consuming practice that would add unduly to the burdens of

Congress. The chief trouble with it seems to lie in the impossibility of confining questions to matters really worth attention. An enormous mass of triviality must be endured. Also the tricky question is hard to escape, the question not put in good faith with an honest intent to get information, but shrewdly devised for personal or political embarrassment.

Were it likely that a daily Question Calendar would secure more of public attention to the proceedings of House and Senate, it might to that extent be a good thing; but as newspaper readers are now generally supposed to demand nothing but the abnormal and to shy at anything instructive, only the amusing or irritating questions and the clever replies would reach the readers of other than the few journals that still run the risk of boring the public. The real value of the information, then, would be mainly within the chamber. But in view of the fact that debate rarely affects votes in Congress, the chamber itself is not the effective place for information. Where it counts, where it is all-important, is in the committee room. There heads of departments or their representatives get a patient, welcome hearing, usually generous and sympathetic. With reasonable accuracy it may be said that no important bill is reported to either branch of Congress until after the views of the branch of the administration concerned have been thus obtained and considered.

One distinct advantage of this method over that which the reformers advocate in the shape of attendance of secretaries at sessions of House and Senate, springs from the fact that secretaries rarely have that familiarity with details of administration which is natural to the assistant secretaries and the bureau chiefs. While a secretary could defend or denounce the broad principle of a proposal affecting his department, he might easily get tangled if questioned on details, and to details questions would largely be addressed. In the committee room the man from the department who knows most about the particular question, either does most of the talking or sits beside his chief and furnishes any facts his superior may lack. Were the secretary to go on the floor of House or Senate, of course the rule might allow him to take in a subordinate official just as the chairman of a committee may have its clerk by his side when a measure it has reported comes up for debate; but the clerk may not address the body, whereas in the committee room anybody may be heard.

With the committee the conference is much less formal and artificial than debate in the chamber must necessarily be. The secretary, his representative, or a bureau chief, will talk in the conversational manner, freely, frankly, and, if unused to

LEADERSHIP

speech-making, without the awkwardness and embarrassment that make many a novice ineffective when on his feet before a sizeable audience. There is no playing to the galleries, for there are no galleries. Nothing is said for political effect, rarely anything for public consumption. Each committee member asks as many questions as he pleases, which usually clarifies the doubtful points. The questions are not asked with ulterior purpose, but with the sole intent of getting the facts.

The testimony, questions and all, is taken down in shorthand, the transcript of which goes to the department for correction and for the insertion of letters, tables of statistics, or other pertinent matter too long or technical to have been read to the committee. Before the bill takes final shape, the printed report of the hearings is available for any committee member to refresh his memory, or to inform himself if he was absent from the hearing. It is also at the command of the corresponding committee in the other branch, thus often saving the repetition of testimony that would otherwise be necessary, and by so much lessening the time taken from the administrative officials concerned.

Is this not a more systematic, thorough, and adequate way of conveying information than the conditions of debate on the floor of House and Senate would make possible if secretaries were to attend the deliberations of those bodies?

116 CONGRESS—AN EXPLANATION

It is interesting to observe that, while the attendance of cabinet officers is being pressed in this country, it is losing favor in the land of its origin. Of late years attendance by members of the English government has dwindled greatly. Perhaps members of the government feel that they cannot spare the time; but a more likely reason is that the concentration of power which is the inevitable development of the cabinet system, has brought the inevitable result — indifference. When difficult revolt against official leadership is the only recourse open to dissatisfied members of the majority, why bother with explanations and answers? "Don't talk! Vote!" Every session of our national House already sees this spirit put into action in the case of some of the most important measures. They will be handled under special rules limiting the time for debate so that it is little more than a farce. Were the administration also to dominate the legislative branch, the baneful effects of this sort of thing would be yet more common.

Apart from their desire for more control from without Congress, American critics urge more of leadership from within. Whenever some opinionated group fails to secure the passage of some pet measure, you are likely to read newspaper editorials, or letters "To the Editor," scoring Congress for lack of leadership. Yet it exists, though perhaps to-day not in the desirable degree. Let it not be forgotten that only fifteen years ago the country was distressed because in the House there was said to be too much leadership. Observation of the way things go now leads me to doubt if net gain has come from the revolt of the so-called insurgents then. In the lack of personal familiarity with the old régime (commonly known as "Cannonism," by reason of its course under Speaker Cannon) comparison may be made with no great confidence; but judging by report, the most striking difference between the old and the new methods is that, whereas leadership was then in the open, it is now under cover. Then the Speaker was the recognized centre of authority. Now nobody knows who in the last resort decides. There is a Committee on Rules, the chairman of which evidently has much influence. Behind this is a steering committee of the majority party, which is supposed to advise. And each party has a floor leader who guides in matters of technical detail, though as a matter of fact most of the floor work is handled by committee chairmen as the measures in their charge come along for action. It might be said that nowadays the leadership of the House is in commission, with the membership of the commission more or less fluctuating and shadowy.

There is no ground for saying that so far the change has distinctly impaired the efficiency of the

House, but it may be submitted that the situation is full of the elements of trouble. Should there be a revival of partisanship in the country at large, with clear-cut issues once more dividing people and Congress into bitterly hostile camps, the present system is not likely to meet the needs of a turbulent House by securing in the majority party the control of its processes and the effective handling of the situation. The division of responsibility between a two-party Rules Committee and a one-party Steering Committee is reasonably sure to make trouble sooner or later. And the same is true of the like division of it between the Speaker and the floor leader. So far things have gone along with tolerable smoothness by reason of the happy chance that has filled these positions with men tactful and conciliatory, capable of working in harmony; but experience does not encourage the hope that such conditions will always prevail. The masterful, dominant leadership of some one man may yet be required.

Probably in such a contingency the party caucus will again amount to something. For a decade it has been of no consequence on the Republican side, rarely meeting and never importantly affecting the action of the House. Results of caucus action have been more evident on the Democratic side, but, at any rate in the last six years, have had no serious influence either on House action or on party for-

LEADERSHIP

tunes. As things stand now, the caucus need not be taken into account when seeking the causes of congressional inefficiency or the sources of congressional achievement.

Whether the caucus functions or not, whether leadership in either branch is strong or weak, criticism is sure to continue because the basic cause for it will persist with anybody's handling of the work under the conditions sure to continue. The trouble comes not over the things done but over the things left undone. Toward the close of the session the congestion of work makes preference inevitable. This means that certain bills will not reach the President. Their friends will feel aggrieved, no matter who made the decision or why it was made, and complaint of bad leadership will follow. With the volume of work forced on Congress, no cure-all presents itself. Time-saving changes in the rules would help, and constant pressure from a leader might induce earlier committee reports, but it will still be true that important bills take long in preparation, and that as the fore part of every session must be mainly devoted to preliminary work, the latter part must see much of the fruition of that work. As the harvesting season taxes the farmer, so the closing weeks of a session tax the legislator. From blame for the mischief that follows, no leader and no form of leadership can escape.

Observation of what takes place in the closing days of a session is likely to strengthen doubt of gain from one-man dominance. Then a fundamental defect is clearly disclosed. Conditions put the life of every measure at the mercy of some one man. If it be a measure of importance, the President is likely to be consulted, and if he objects to giving it a chance, it will be erased from the programme. Or the power to discard may be exercised by the chairman of the Committee on Rules, effectively even if sometimes indirectly. The Speaker can refuse to recognize the would-be mover of the necessary motion. Nothing is likely to prevail against the wishes of the majority leader in House or Senate. The minority leader in the House can start a compelling filibuster, and any one Senator can interpose the same obstacle. The minor measures are taken up only by unanimous consent, so that one man can block any of them he disapproves.

This, it will be seen, puts the negative decision in the control of some one individual, which is directly contrary to the spirit of democratic institutions. Their theory is that either the adoption or the rejection of any legislative proposal shall result from the consensus of many minds, being more than half of those entrusted with the responsibility under the forms of representative government. The wisdom of this theory is emphatically shown by instances

LEADERSHIP

frequent in the last week of every session when legislation wished by the majority is thwarted through the prejudice, narrowness, stupidity, misinformation, or sheer ignorance of some one man.

If it be urged that the remedy is to concentrate the power of rejection in a leader, autocrat, dictator, czar, or whatever you may call him, then it is to be pointed out that, although the weaknesses of human nature are not apt to be so prominent in the man likely to be chosen or accepted, as in some others of the many now clothed with the power, yet no mortal is wholly without these weaknesses. It is partly because of this that nowadays we have legislative assemblies instead of lawgiving monarchs.

Turning from the negative to the affirmative phase of the problem, a better argument may be made for autocratic leadership. When the scarcity of time compels choice between measures competing for the right of way, and to prefer some does not necessarily compel the rejection of others, it may be that resort to an arbiter will serve a useful purpose and be accompanied by no great danger. Yet it is doubtful if at that stage any method of decision will secure in full the results to be desired. The trouble is that no one man is likely to have the needed range of knowledge and breadth of vision. The thing to be determined is not intrinsic merit, but relative merit. That question is now first raised. There is no time for thorough comparisons, for the weighing of arguments. The arbiter can profit little by advice, for the issue will be as novel to everybody else as to himself, and counsellors are as unlikely as he himself is either to have balanced information or to form unprejudiced judgment. There are at hand no measuring standards. Generally the competing proposals have no common factor that can be scaled. How will a man set about determining forthwith whether more good will accrue from developing the merchant marine than from reforming the methods of criminal justice; whether it is more desirable to encourage coöperative marketing than to provide additional hospitals for disabled veterans?

Evidently reliance upon any one man in such a juncture is not the ideal course. It cannot be wholly escaped, but its defects can be lessened in volume by trying to anticipate them. This can be done by giving the forces of public opinion time enough to play their natural and legitimate part, which will be possible when there is more attempt than now to reach agreement in advance as to what achievements are most to be desired. If congressional leadership could be developed along that line, we might have much more of valuable constructive action. Under such leadership we should have a legislative programme decided upon early in the session, with a few really important objectives to be

LEADERSHIP 123

kept constantly in mind. This is the sort of thing the country wants, if we may judge from the attention and respect paid to what have come to be known as "the President's policies." They have at least quasi-constitutional recognition in the power given to the President to recommend. Notice the distinction between this power and that of what is inaccurately called the veto. The President cannot in fact forbid, he can only ask Congress to reconsider, and with a two thirds vote it prevails. But there is no limitation on his power to recommend. The difference in authority was prudent. It recognized the difference between affirmative and negative power, between construction and obstruction, between safe leadership and dangerous leadership. Here once again the wisdom of the men who wrote the Constitution may point the way to meet the problems of to-day.

Lecture V

CRITICISM AND REMEDY

POSSIBLY Congress is in greater disfavor to-day than at any previous period of its history. The same thing may be true of the state legislatures. It is said to be true of Parliament and of the older assemblies of the European Continent. Indeed it is a world-wide phenomenon. To try to learn the cause and the remedy is worth while.

Let the inquiry be prefaced by observing that criticism of lawmakers and of laws is, always has been, and doubtless always will be a favorite occupation of mankind. Because government is the most important of earthly pursuits, naturally it is in the matter of government that men most often voice their discontent. For the same reason, laws and lawmaking and lawmakers and all they involve are the most common theme of those who by pen or voice share in forming public judgments, and as fault-finding is more interesting and marketable than praise, the critics who blame get the wider hearing or reading. Beware lest they make you forget that there may be another side to the argument.

CRITICISM AND REMEDY 125

Keep in mind certain traits of human nature. Some men think that whatever is, is wrong; they are blind to any virtue that exists. Others always find distant hills the greenest; to them Arcadia is beyond the sea. Many are sure that the past was better than the present; in those days there were demigods.

Such considerations may account for that part of the criticism which can be matched by like criticism in all ages of all lands; but beyond it, must be recognized widespread belief by fair, candid, normal men that there has been deterioration in lawmaking bodies, and that representative institutions as we know them approach failure. What has produced this belief?

First may be named discontent with results. Democracy has disappointed. It has not brought the millennium. Millions of men have failed to get from it that bettering of their condition which they hoped. Faith has given place to doubt. Herein lies an explanation that appeals to President Lowell observing the United States, to H. G. Wells observing Great Britain, each familiar with what is going on in the rest of the world.

The volume of individual discontent has been vastly increased in the last seventy-five years by the spread of what we commonly call education, when we have in mind the schooling that now lets men and women by the million acquire information of a sort and absorb miscellaneous opinion. The bulk of this comes to them through those newspapers that emphasize the abnormal things in life, and the abnormal is that which is contrary to law, whether it be the unwritten law of customs, habits, and manners that makes up probably nine tenths of the inhibitions on personal conduct, or the written law brought into play to supplement the unwritten law in the matter of the other tenth. The public school has greatly enlarged the number of those who habitually read books, and the spread of public libraries has furnished the opportunity to get books, with the circulation predominantly that of fiction, where again the abnormal prevails, popularity being more or less in proportion to improbability. Of late the moving pictures have added their influence to the cult of the abnormal. All this has contributed to break down the respect for that in life which is normal, natural, customary, lawful.

Particularly influential in the matter of the public attitude toward its lawmakers and administrative officials has been the course of the press. Half a century ago it was possible to find in many journals a reasonably thorough, dignified, and instructive report of legislative proceedings, adequately informing the public of what took place, with an attention to proportion meant to satisfy an intelligent reader

CRITICISM AND REMEDY 127

interested in public affairs. To-day such a report is rare. With but few exceptions the larger papers will not give it space. They will print only the spectacular matter, or that which pertains to topics presumed to have unusual popular interest. Legislating is rarely dramatic. Having learned that more money is to be made by entertainment than by instruction, most publishers of course follow the more attractive path. The result is that the amusing, the undignified, the foolish doings of lawmakers and incidents of lawmaking are "played up."

For illustration, take the absurd bills sure to be introduced. The newspaper story never explains that the theory of representative institutions contemplates an opportunity for every citizen to present his grievance and suggest a remedy. There are silly citizens. When one comes to his Representative with his pet notion, shall it be refused a hearing? You may say that a Representative ought to decline to present such measures. He usually does, but now and then an honest and not altogether illogical belief that every petitioner ought to be heard, leads to the introduction of a bill with which the member introducing has not the slightest sympathy. Occasionally, too, a constituency will elect for its Representative a half-insane man, who will introduce a preposterous bill of his own. Nearly all the fool propositions, however, come from outside. Surely it is not fair to judge a lawmaking body by such things, and yet their exploitation in the press contributes not a little to the poor opinion in which all legislators are held.

It is the exceptional lawmaker, too, who furnishes grist for the humorist. "Senator Sorghum" is a favorite character in the funny columns. Nobody in Washington knows him. I recall no Senator and no Representative who in mannerisms resembles him. Of course there are men in Congress who have peculiarities of speech or conduct, just as would be found among an equal number of jurists, physicians, architects, merchants; but there are very few who do not observe all the usual conventions. There is absolutely no warrant for making the typical Congressman the butt of ridicule. Yet if you will watch the pages of such a periodical as "Life" while Congress is in session, you will find nearly every number containing somewhere from five to twenty flings at the expense of the nation's lawmakers. The persistence of this sort of thing in the press, day in and day out, year after year, helps shape the public appraisal.

On the other hand, the earnest, serious, valuable work of Congress, and of the legislatures also, is for the most part ignored. The same thing is true of the administrative field of public service. The ordinary, habitual contributions of public servants to the

CRITICISM AND REMEDY

common welfare get scant notice, but their follies, errors, and crimes are blazoned abroad. Is it not inevitable that the people should have a distorted idea of public life?

Another influence of the press shows itself in the matter of what may be called transient public opinion. Nowadays those journals seeking or having the larger circulations, counting or hoping to count their readers by hundreds of thousands, find it profitable to play on passion or prejudice by championing this or that social, economic, or political fad of the moment. The thoughtless men who act from impulse, and promptly reach emphatic conclusions after reading but one side of a question, demand that a new law be enacted straight off. Congress, slow and cautious, fails to respond and is forthwith condemned by the impatient multitude. A few months later the fad may be forgotten, but the mental impression of indifference and lethargy remains.

Next we must reckon with the effect of the material and social changes of the last two generations. The growth of wealth has affected the standing of legislative bodies through exposing them to more powerful influences of a selfish nature than the world has seen since the decadent days of the Roman Senate. The corporate form of commercial activity lends itself peculiarly to methods that eliminate the restraining power of individual conscience. Also, through the money at command, it has made possible an unprecedented development of the art of propaganda, by which an artificial opinion may be created for the purpose of accomplishing selfish ends. The associations and organizations of many kinds that have had of late such phenomenal growth have resorted to like methods.

The device tends not only to muddle public opinion itself, but also to vitiate the processes we have developed for putting opinion into action. The indications are that there is decidedly less venality in elections and in public life than half a century ago; but as one form of dangerous influence has waned, another has grown. To-day the menace comes from organized faction, whether corporate or otherwise massed. Washington now contains the headquarters of many such factions, some of them occupying pretentious buildings of their own, some claiming to speak for millions of voters. Their legislative agents are often capable and well-paid, and as their positions depend on getting results, they are a real factor. The old-time lobbyist has gone, but the new brand, though more respectable, has perhaps a more damaging effect by working on the timidity of lawmakers rather than on their cupidity.

Furthermore, the progress of science by leaps and bounds has brought to lawmaking bodies a great

CRITICISM AND REMEDY

variety of problems calling for technical knowledge that cannot be adequately supplied by representatives chosen for the most part with no regard to special training. Public life rarely attracts experts. Neither does it often enlist exceptional men of affairs. In our legislative bodies lawyers still predominate, and being mostly lawyers from towns and the smaller cities, they rarely have had training and experience fitting them to cope with the big constructive problems in the administrative field of present-day government.

In quite another direction scientific and mechanical progress has had important political consequence in a way not generally understood. The development of transportation and communication, the steam locomotive, the electric motor, the automobile, the telegraph, the telephone, and lately the radio, have greatly broadened the scope of human relationships. The boundaries of village, town, city, or even a state, no longer confine anybody's interests. The inevitable consequence has been to widen the circles of legislation. The town-meeting has dwindled in importance because the town can no longer live unto itself alone. Home rule for cities is a losing cry because millions who dwell outside the cities are almost as much concerned in their affairs as those who elect the city councils. The state legislatures, flooded with problems that once were local and left to localities, find some relief in the transfer of old tasks to the national government. Deplore it as much as we please, resist it as stoutly as we can, centralization marches on. It may be delayed, but it cannot be stopped.

Congress suffers most, because there is no place higher up to which it can turn for relief. Its old labors remain while the new ones are added. Note a part of the legislative tasks forced on Congress from below in the last half century as suggested by the names of some of the resulting agencies: the Interstate Commerce Commission, the Federal Reserve Board, the Federal Farm Loan Bureau, the Bureau of Education, the Prohibition Commissioner, the Public Health Service, the Militia Bureau, the Bureau of Mines, the National Park Service, the Forest Service (not to specify a dozen other Bureaus of the Agricultural Department), the Children's Bureau, the Women's Bureau, the Railroad Labor Board, the Federal Trade Commission, the Federal Power Commission. Congress has not wrenched these things from the states. The people of the states have driven Congress to take them over, reluctantly, regretfully. No thoughtful man can watch the workings of a centralized government at close range, as every Congressman must do (if for no other reason than that of his presence in Washington), without regret and anxiety. But the stubborn

CRITICISM AND REMEDY

facts of social and economic change must be accepted. Congress is not to be blamed for them, nor can it fairly be criticized if it has not proved fully equal to the tremendous increase in its responsibilities.

Another of these stubborn facts is the ever-growing demand for the use of the powers of government to protect the weak against the strong. Of course, the strong resent this and call it invasion of personal liberty. The strong man thinks he has an inherent right to make, buy, or sell what he pleases; to employ others on his own terms and discharge them when it suits him; to acquire all the property he can, use it in any way that fancy dictates while he is alive, and direct the disposition of it all after his death. He believes it his right to drive his automobile as fast as he may wish, to shoot, hunt, fish, and ride anywhere. When by brute force he can deprive another of property, we go so far as to call him a criminal. When within the letter of the law he does the same thing by the use of his wits, and the victim resents it, the strong man laughs. If his passions or his appetites harm others, nevertheless he thinks himself within his unalienable right to the pursuit of his own happiness.

The masses of mankind, helpless through ages to resist the tyrannies of the strong few, have now in their hands a weapon of defence — the ballot —

which gives them a chance to make protective law. Perhaps they are wielding that weapon clumsily, but wield it they will. They mean to defend themselves if they can against the grafter, the exploiter, the extortioner, the usurer; against the seller of rum, cocaine, and every other kind of poison; against the gambler and the cheat. To their demands lawmakers of every grade must now at least listen, to an extent never before known. The granting of some part of these demands, those that have seemed reasonable to the lawmakers, has aroused the wrath of many men thereby deprived of the privilege of advantaging themselves by hurting others. Hence no small part of the current criticism of law and lawmaking and lawmakers.

The criticism showered on Congress and the legislatures may be of itself one cause for more criticism. Surely it does not encourage promising young men to choose public life as a career. On the other hand, may it not actually deter men young or old who are jealous of their reputations and loath to invite obloquy? I am not ready to admit that our representatives, state and national, are less capable, honorable, or unselfish than their predecessors. If judgment can safely be based on recorded ridicule and opprobrium, there has on the contrary been distinct gain in the character and quality of representatives. This in some measure ought to have

CRITICISM AND REMEDY 135

come about as the result of the increase in schooling, which has markedly enlarged the percentage of what we call educated men in the community, the class from which representatives are chiefly drawn. Furthermore those who have not had many years in school are far better informed than were their fathers, by reason of the press and other facilities for the diffusion of knowledge. With a wider range for appropriate choice, we ought to have, and probably do have, a higher average of informed intelligence in our legislative chambers than ever before. If it is still below what might be fairly expected, the disrepute of lawmaking may be one cause. Alone, however, it would hardly explain the situation. Reasons must also be sought in other directions.

Possibly the search will lead us to fundamentals. It may be that the fault is in methods of selection of representatives, or, more broadly, in the accustomed structure of representative government.

Methods of selection are still in process of development. We are yet in the experimental stage. There is no proof that the various extensions of the suffrage have contributed anything toward more satisfactory government, whatever may have been their indirect advantages. The preliminary processes, those of nomination, have made gain by changes from time to time, but the most recent, the primary, is evidently only a step toward something better. What form election methods will next take must be worked out by experience. Meanwhile some helps are at hand. The most promising of them is the gradual restricting of the use of money. Surely, even if it be slowly, public opinion is coming to frown on campaign expenditures. The latest presidential campaign showed no small gain in this particular. The change in opinion is reflected in the laws that little by little are shifting the cost of nominations and elections to the public treasury. If the next forty years see as much progress as the last forty, 1965 will find the whole cost borne as it ought to be, by the taxpayers, and private outlay will have disappeared. Election to office is a public, not a private concern, and individuals have no business to vitiate by the use of money the ascertainment of the public will.

Another help appears in the greater willingness of the electorate to continue representatives in office. This the primary election system has made easier— a merit in that system which alone is important enough to offset sundry defects. It has shown that the mass of the voters do not really want that rotation in office so much favored by little politicians. Also the visible merits of civil service reform in practice have contributed to develop public sympathy with the idea of long public service. It begins to look as if presently it may be as natural and easy

CRITICISM AND REMEDY 137

for a man to make public service his profession as it long has been to pursue a career in any field of private service. Once this is established, it is certain that many young men will deliberately and hopefully train themselves for public life, with as much benefit to public life as to themselves.

Then will disappear the dwindling heresy that public office should seek the man and not the man the office. It is a heresy that has never prevailed in any part of the world except the northeastern quarter of the United States, but hereabouts it has had mischievous strength. Fortunately we are now coming to realize that ambition to serve one's fellows is just as honorable in the field of government as in that of religion or medicine or any other altruistic calling. We shall presently admit, even in New England, that it is as proper to aspire to make laws as it long has been to aspire to interpret laws. When legislative schools stand on an equal footing with law schools, the country will have better lawmakers.

Helpful as progress in such particulars will be, it may prove only a palliative. Possibly the ailment needs more drastic treatment, going to the root of the trouble. It may be that only radical alteration of our present representative system can meet the new situation. The suggestion does not impeach the wisdom of the men who framed our Constitution.

For the conditions of the time that instrument was a miracle of sagacity. The conditions have changed. From a fairly homogeneous people numbering a few millions in a comparatively small area, we have become a singularly heterogeneous people of many millions occupying a vast country. At the same time economic and social relations and needs have altogether changed. It may be that a system of representation based on numbers or areas, that is to say, arithmetical or geographical, no longer suffices, and that to its insufficiency may be traced the cause for complaints usually met by more superficial explanations.

There is ground for prediction that along this line there will be development. The most interesting and perhaps the most promising movement of the sort now in sight appears in some of the newer constitutions of Continental Europe in the shape of provisions looking to the representation of interests, of groups and classes, in addition to the familiar numerical and geographical representation. In Germany this has been carried to the point of establishing a wholly new and distinct assembly, made up of representatives of a large variety of industrial, commercial, and other economic groups, which is functioning alongside of and in conjunction with the usual lawmaking body.

In our own country proposals for structural or

CRITICISM AND REMEDY 139

technical changes furnish less hope of speedy headway. Group representation has been attempted in Congress by the formation of one disturbing faction, the agricultural bloc; but the probability is that, even if it holds together at all, it will not continue to be an important factor. It is inconsistent with the two-party system that English-speaking people believe to be more satisfactory than the many-party system in vogue on the Continent.

Structural change of the national government in our time being practically out of the question, Congress will not be touched by any discussion of the unicameral system. For the same reason, the agitation for reducing the size of legislative houses almost to the commission form, which has not yet wholly died out in some of our Western states, has no practical pertinence in connection with Congress. Some argument is heard for cutting down the membership of the national House of Representatives, now 435, to, say, 300, but it may be safely predicted that this will not be done. Indeed, those who believe the present membership too unwieldy will be fortunate if they prevent increase the next time an apportionment bill is passed.

There are two sides to this question of the size of the House. The public rarely hears of but one, for the critics seem to take it for granted that outside Congress itself the arguments are all one way, and so only half the story gets into print. It is true that the floor work of the House might go somewhat better if the membership were smaller; but inasmuch as most of it is done anyhow with an attendance of only a few score, that consideration is after all not so very important. Moreover, it is outweighed by the fact that the really effective work of Congressmen is done mostly in the committee rooms. This means a subdivision of labor that might not be helped if there were fewer members among whom to apportion the tasks. Then, too, reducing the membership would proportionately add to individual office work. As it is now, each member is in effect a liaison officer linking on the average about 260,000 persons with the administrative functions of the national government. To reduce the membership to 300 would make each member the helper of about 380,000 persons. A theorist would say that this consideration ought not to exist. Perhaps so, but it does exist, and it is not illegitimate either. In a thousand ways the member of Congress can be of perfectly proper help to his constituents, furnishing them information that will save them time and expense, putting them in quick touch with the right administrative officials, suggesting how best to get grievances duly considered, securing and distributing public documents so that they will do the most good, presenting the needs of localities in respect of

CRITICISM AND REMEDY 141

the various public services, preparing private bills to meet the claims of deserving persons who may be indigent. Then there are the personal courtesies that visitors to Washington may properly expect from their Representatives. To be sure, provision is made for much of the routine of all this by furnishing secretaries and clerks at public expense; yet the member must give no small part of it his personal attention, at least to the extent of oversight; and of course, the more of it there is, the greater the demands on his time and strength. It is a load that grows both with the growth of population and with the spread of governmental functions. To meet it by lessening the number of men among whom it may be divided is hardly logical. Such recourse is not to be expected from those who know best what it means.

Reform by way of limiting the length or frequency of sessions is another proposal that may be summarily dismissed as far as Congress is concerned. It is purely a state issue, for there is no likelihood whatever that the people of the Union as a whole will in our day be so foolish as to try to get more work by lessening the time and opportunity. Another cure-all, the Initiative and Referendum, is likely to continue to be a state concern, in spite of the attempt by some of the radical conservatives to apply the Referendum part of it to amendments proposed to the Federal Constitution. Nobody yet suggests that it be used to weaken the backbone of Congress.

Such remedies do not go to the heart of the difficulty. They would not reach the chief source of trouble in our lawmaking bodies, state and national. The real cause is the attempt to do more work than can be well done under present conditions. We have been blind to what has been brought about by the growth of population; by the march of science; by the triumphs of invention; by the economic and social changes of the last fifty years. We vainly try to cope with the results by the use of machinery long outgrown. Because of an exaggerated respect for precedent, or of inertia or timidity, we refuse to scrap that part of the machinery which no longer accomplishes a useful purpose and we refuse to adjust the rest of it to modern conditions.

When a manufacturer finds that he can no longer handle the work pressed upon him, he will either tune up his machinery so that with the same plant he can turn out more product, or he will add more plant. Either or both of these things can be done with the machinery of legislation. Without doing any person or any interest serious harm, the procedure of Congress could be so improved along lines already thoroughly tested by other important legislative bodies, that one third more work could be

CRITICISM AND REMEDY 143

done in the time now consumed. Or by using methods familiar in England and on the Continent of Europe, enough work might be shifted from Congress to other agencies so that Congress could probably handle with ease all that would remain.

England has met the situation, at least in part, by the development of what is known as the Provisional Order System. Eighty years ago the relief of Parliament began by starting to let administrative departments attend to details. Gradually it became more and more common to confine statutes to general principles, and to authorize departments to apply these principles, and to supplement broad commands with needed rules and regulations. By 1893 the transfer of subordinate lawmaking to administrative boards had reached the point where it was advisable to publish the annual grist of Statutory Orders separately from the Public General Acts. Now these orders make a volume, sometimes two volumes, much thicker than that other volume which astonishes an American when he is told it contains all the general laws enacted in a year for the vast British Empire. In 1920 there were 82 Acts of Parliament, but there were more than 800 Statutory Rules and Orders issued, occupying about three thousand pages.

Parliament delegates legislative power in four ways. Not always with logical precision, yet with some approach to due proportion, the trivial things are put within the complete control of the administrative departments; the rules of somewhat more importance take effect at once, subject to annulment by Parliament within a specified time, usually twenty-one sitting days, though the number of days specified may be as high as one hundred; the rules of still more importance take effect after the time specified, if meanwhile Parliament has not taken action to the contrary; and the rules of yet greater importance take effect when Parliament consents. It is not uncommon to find as many as sixty sets of rules in the list laid before the members. They are seldom killed. Those to which Parliament must give positive approval are grouped each year into a series of consolidated measures known as Provisional Orders Confirmation Acts, and are passed through the usual stages of legislation. It has been computed that in forty years less than one per cent of such orders have been rejected by Parliament.

The principle involved in the delegation of minor lawmaking has in our own country been familiar from the earliest days. It appears in the ordinances and by-laws of villages, towns, cities, and counties, wherever such are found, the authority having been delegated by the legislatures. The states, however, have been most reluctant to delegate to

CRITICISM AND REMEDY 145

any agency save their subdivisions, though of late years more or less of the rule-making power has almost unconsciously been entrusted to administrative boards of one sort or another. Like conditions have driven Congress in the same direction, but there, as in the state legislatures, the dread of bureaucracy is very strong. Unrestricted delegation has indeed serious menace, for to clothe a single official or a small group of public servants with the power to make law, especially if penalties go along with it, opens the door for all sorts of injustice and oppression. The danger in this direction seems to be minimized, if not altogether removed, by the English device of confirmation or its opportunity.

Should Congress see fit to profit by the experience of Parliament in this matter, it could save a great amount of time. You will observe that under the Provisional Order system, the task of framing the law is performed outside Parliament. With us the positive steps are taken by the committee and then by the House to which it reports. It is the constructive action that most invites unnecessary discussion. Vetoes are rarely debated, and though confirmation is not on exactly the same footing with a veto coming from outside, yet it may be safely predicted that neither confirming nor the opportunity to demand it would arouse anything like the discussion now inevitable as the minutiæ of legislation come along.

Congress could wisely at once get rid of no insignificant part of its labors if it would apply the Provisional Order system to such matters as the affairs of the District of Columbia, bridge bills, pensions, correction of military records, much other private legislation, and the major part of the details incident to the administration of revenue laws, banking laws, and indeed most of the other laws that concern simply the machinery of government.

What possible objection could there be to applying this system forthwith to the affairs of what is officially known as the District of Columbia, unofficially known as the city of Washington? Alone of all the cities in the land, it does not govern itself. There are valid and sufficient reasons for not giving it self-government. Congress should and will control its affairs. But it is absurd that the initiative in many of its trivial matters should be confined to a congressional committee. What harm could result if ordinances and budgets and the other details elsewhere entrusted fully to city councils, should here be prepared by the District Commissioners or some group especially chosen for the purpose, to take effect if not vetoed or modified by Congress within a fixed time? In view of local conditions, it might be particularly fortunate if such an initiating body were selected after the fashion winning favor in some of the large Massachusetts towns that do

CRITICISM AND REMEDY 147

not want to take on the usual form of city government. In Washington it might well be a body of several hundred men and women named from every kind of serious organization in the city. As such a body would doubtless work through a reasonably small executive committee, with its recommendations passed upon by the full body, the result ought to be a well-digested programme embodying the wishes of the citizens as a whole.

Such a programme would relieve Congress to a degree not indeed great, yet worth while. The House now undertakes by rule to give to District matters two days of each month — about one twelfth of the session. This is not enough for the District and is too much for the House. Both would gain if 435 men from all parts of this great country were not asked to act as the council for a city containing less than one half of one per cent of the population of the nation. The simple remedy is for Congress to exercise only the veto power.

Beyond such better utilization of existing plant is the possibility of additional plant, such, for example, as I have referred to in the case of the Federal Economic Council that Germany has created. This establishes alongside the usual legislating body a group made representative on a different basis, which can prepare and submit drafts of laws in the economic field under conditions likely to secure speedy acceptance. As a device for the authoritative preparation of laws it will be worth watching and, perhaps, copying.

Of a kindred nature is the use of special commissions for preliminary study of complicated questions. Such commissions are already a common resort of some at least of the state legislatures, but as yet have been little used by Congress. That body seems not to know how to profit by them. For instance, the extensive, costly, and valuable work of the Coal Commission has been ignored. Perhaps one reason for this particular misfortune may be found in the fact that no member of either branch was on the Commission. That was a mistake. The most effective commission is made up partly of legislators and partly of men chosen from private life because of either general capacity or special familiarity with the particular problem. This permits the help of the expert specialist, to furnish technical knowledge; the broad-minded citizen of high repute, not only to contribute sound judgment but also to win public confidence; and the practical legislator, to tell what legislation is possible and to fight for it when it has been recommended. The trouble with a commission made up wholly of outsiders is that it secures the personal interest of no one in the legislative body. Its report may be of great value to students and may help to form public opinion with ultimate effect on legislation, but the chance of immediate result is lessened by the absence of an interested champion in the body to which the report is made. On the other hand, a commission made up wholly of legislators, taking the shape of a special recess committee, fails to get the benefits of expert coöperation and of the wisdom that may be contributed by private citizens recognized as men of exceptional ability. The mixed commission, it may be confidently expected, or at any rate earnestly hoped, will presently come to be more often used to relieve Congress of some of its labors, and at the same time furnish a broader and better foundation for the more important laws.

Congress also has the opportunity to rid itself entirely of some part of its burden by turning it over to existing agencies quite competent to take it without danger to the public treasury or any private interests. This is notably the case in the matter of claims, various classes of which should at once be entrusted to the Court of Claims, or in the minor instances to the departments concerned, perhaps with appeal from them to the Court of Claims. The principle may some day be carried further by the establishment of a permanent administrative body, sitting continuously, after the fashion of the Interstate Commerce Commission, which shall have final authority in respect of at least the minor administrative legislation, and perhaps go the full distance in relieving Congress of all work except the determination of broad policies.

Such a step would be an adoption of business practices in a field where they may properly apply. Congress should not delegate the appropriating of the taxpayer's money; it should still say how much shall be spent and for what purposes; but some day it may decide that it need no longer charge itself with attention to the details of carrying out its policies. Just as the directors of a big corporation safely and usefully leave this to an executive committee, so Congress will then do, though it may not select the committee from its own members. That might be for a constitutional amendment to determine.

Think how many gains would follow if Congress had nothing to do save to determine policies. Membership in it would be so much more attractive that everywhere strong men would aspire to election. The dreadful waste of time on dull minutiæ that now confronts Congress would no longer deter men who so much want to put their energies only into things worth while, that they will not accept a task mostly meticulous.

Those members who care only for the little things of life and those who love petty power might deplore such a change, but the great mass of men elected to Congress would prefer dealing with only big prob-

CRITICISM AND REMEDY 151

lems. The inability to do this now brings the keenest disappointment that comes to the new member. Through his first term he feels himself an insignificant cog in a big machine. Not until he has been there several years, is he likely to feel that he has had a real part in helping to solve any problem involving principle. Even then he will have close relationship to but a few of the big questions. The ablest men in the House rarely take part in debating more than two or three such questions in the course of a session, and then the conditions seldom permit adequate treatment.

To sum it up, there is less opportunity in the national House of Representatives than ever before for the capable man to make the best use of his powers. Unless methods are changed, the situation in this respect is sure to become worse, for a steady increase in the volume of administrative detail is inevitable. The country will keep on growing; its activities, interests, and needs will keep on expanding. So year by year the petty work of a Congressman will become more burdensome, and he will perforce be less and less of a statesman, more and more of a mechanician.

If this diagnosis be accurate, the reason for the growing disrepute of Congress is clear. The people expect their representatives to be statesmen. They want the great questions of policy, in which alone they take interest, to be handled diligently, with reasonably prompt conclusion. They wax impatient over the interminable delays in dealing with such matters as the World Court, the development of aeronautics, the Merchant Marine, Muscle Shoals, enforcement of prohibition, reform of the criminal law to the end that there may be more sure and speedy punishment of lawbreakers. Not knowing why the machinery of Congress is so clogged, they have no mercy on a body that is in fact doing the best it can under the conditions.

Fairer would be the judgment were it based on comparison with the other great legislative bodies of the world. Never were they so generally criticized. The proximate causes vary, but the ultimate cause appears to be common to them all. The old methods of representative government are nowhere equal to the problems springing from the complexities of modern life. We are at least no worse off than the rest. On the contrary, if results are to be measured by peace, contentment, and prosperity, we are better off.

Apart from all questions of task, machinery, methods, and their effect upon product, it is to be said of Congress that as a whole it is a body of patriotic, high-minded, conscientious men, a body not tainted by venality, but honest, sincere, and faithful. Taken individually, some members of course

CRITICISM AND REMEDY 153

will be found with certain qualities not to be commended. In any group of more than five hundred men that is inevitable. The surprising and gratifying thing is that here the percentage of abnormality is so small. Far the greater number of the members are serious, earnest men of sober lives, decent in thought and deed. Many are active in the work of the churches. Not all are saints, and some are sinners, but righteousness is the rule. Most of the members bring their families to Washington and pass quietly with them the hours of leisure. In spite of the impression to the contrary, social distractions are few, and the great mass of the members enjoy little gaiety.

In the performance of their public duties the members show sincerity of purpose in high degree. In the deliberations of the committee room, where men most reveal themselves, unselfish desire to advance the public interest is paramount. The display of genuine patriotism there should convince the sceptic and confound the cynic. The members of Congress give the best that is in them to their country.

Speaker Gillett, who has just left the House after the longest continuous service of any member representing any one district, said when bidding his colleagues farewell: "Possibly the House is not as brilliant as it was thirty years ago. It certainly is not as dissipated. It does more work. And in my opinion, weighing carefully my words, the average ability, industry, and serious devotion to duty is higher to-day than when I came." Adding to this the judgment formed by studying the congressional history of the century before Mr. Gillett became a member, I feel confident in saying that the ethical standards of Congress were never so high as they are now. In point of purpose and endeavor it deserves the trust and approval of the nation.